P   O   E   M   S

PPPPPP

PERFORMANCE

PPPPPP

PIECES

PPPPPP

PPPPPP

PROSES

PPPPPP

PLAYS

PPPPPP

POETICS

In the series

    Border Lines: Works in Translation

A Project of

    the Creative Writing Program at Temple University

    Lawrence Venuti, General Editor

PPPPPP

KURT **SCHWITTERS**

```
P   O   E   M   S
P E R F O R M A N C E S
P   I   E   C   E   S
P   R   O   S   E
P   L   A   Y   S
P O E T I C S
```

edited & translated by   jerome rothenberg & pierre joris

t e m p l e
u n i v e r s i t y
p r e s s
p h i l a d e l p h i a

Temple University Press, Philadelphia 19122 ▐ Copyright © 1993 by Jerome Rothenberg and Pierre Joris ▐ All rights reserved ▐ Published 1993 ▐ Printed in the United States of America ▐ The paper used in this publication is acid free for greater permanence.

Library of Congress Cataloging-in-Publication-Data ▐ Schwitters, Kurt, 1887–1948. ▐ [Selections. English. 1993] ▐ Poems, performance pieces, proses, plays, poetics. ▐ Kurt Schwitters; edited and translated by Jerome Rothenberg & Pierre Joris. ▐ p. cm. —(Border lines) ▐ Translation of selections from: Das literarische Werk. ▐ Includes index. ▐ ISBN 0-87722-894-9 ▐ 1. Schwitters, Kurt, 1887–1948—Translations into English. ▐ I. Rothenberg, Jerome, 1931–. ▐ II. Joris, Pierre, 1946–. ▐ III. Title. ▐ IV. Title: Poems, performance pieces, proses, plays, poetics. ▐ V. Series: Border lines: works in translation (Philadelphia, Pa.) ▐ PT2638.W896A27 ▐ 1993 ▐ 831'.912–dc20 ▐ 92-17365 ▐ CIP Rev.

The chronology of Schwitters' life, which appears in translation at the end of this volume, is taken from Werner Schmalenbach, *Kurt Schwitters,* Prestel-Verlag, Munich, reprinted 1984, and is used here with the kind permission of the publisher.

Permission to reprint the excerpt from the poem by Charles Olson has been generously granted by the Regents of the University of California. The poem appears in Charles Olson, *The Maximus Poems,* edited by George Butterick. Copyright © 1983 The Regents of the University of California, and published by the University of California Press.

All rights in all countries for the original German edition —Kurt Schwitters, *Das literarische Werk*, edited by Friedhelm Lach—are held by DuMont Buchverlag GmbH & Co., Kommanditgesellschaft, Cologne, Germany.

SHORT BIOGRAPHY 1939*

*I was born a very small child. My mother gave me as a present to my father, to make him rejoice. When my father found out that I was a man, he couldn't control himself, and jumped for joy all over the room, for all his life he had only wished for men. But for my father the greatest joy was that I was not a twin.

Then I grew up to be the joy of other people, and throughout my life it has always been my endeavor to create joy for other people. If they get upset at times, that's not my fault. My teacher always enjoyed slapping me, and the whole school rejoiced when I was finally done with it.

Contents

xv Introduction

POEMS & PERFORMANCE PIECES
3   The World
3   Unstupid
4   Nights
5   "Thou"
5   Legborders
6   Green Child
9   Wound roses roses bleed
10 Light & Low
11 Cnudgel
12 Madd Madd World
13 He She It
14 Simultaneous Poem
14 Repose
15 An Anna Blume
16 Anna Blossom Has Wheels
17 Call It Killing You Off
18 The Bahnhof
18 Execution
19 To Johannes Molzahn
20 Herwarth Walden
20 Portrait of Herwarth Walden
21 Portrait of Nell Walden
21 Portrait of Christof Spengemann
22 Portrait of Rudolf Blümner
22 Portrait of Rudolf Bauer
23 Mary the Red
23 To Maria
24 On a Drawing by Marc Chagall
25 A Flower Like a Raven
25 Private Gentlemen, Attention Please!

26	Decay's Way
26	Wheelers Dealers
27	Evening
27	Waggling
28	From the Back & from the Front to Start
29	Murder Machine 43
32	Chinese Banalities
33	The Prisoner
34	Workers Song
35	Subway Poem
35	High Fashion Furs
36	Raspberry Bonbons
36	The Meadow
37	The Critic
38	For Franz Marc
38	The Great Ardor of Dada
40	Cigarren
41	Simile
41	Your Most Humble
42	To the Berlin Proletariat!
42	Desire
43	Candle Fat
43	Ice Clocks
44	Village Poem
44	Dumb Poem
45	Wirecircus
45	The Hand
46	Analysis
46	Roses abloom like daisy blossoms
47	Autumn
47	Twelve
48	Poem 25
49	Z A
49	Register
50	Typographic Visual Poem
50	AO Visual Poem

51	A-A Visual Poem
51	S-S Visual Poem
52	Ur Sonata
81	Indecent i-Poem
81	p p p p p p p p p
82	Banalities (1) and (2)
85	From *Hannover Merzbau*
86	[1 7 10]
87	Ideas for Poems
88	Autumn / The Last Fly
89	Four Bear Songs
91	Tortrtalt
92	Devil in Need
93	For Anne: A Poem to Be Sung as a Round
94	If I Were, When I Was
facing 94	Four Visual Poems: Mai 191, Oon, Difficult, Esir
95	Premonitions
95	When someone once said
96	Small Chinese Poem
96	Flight
99	Perhaps Strange
100	There was a little Kew
101	Imagination
101	Funeral Furnitures at your service
102	She Dolls with Dollies
102	Königsberger Is Like That
103	Dadar
103	I and You
104	[Frohe Tage]
106	And in the night
106	She is my fairy queen
107	Count Sardinowhocount
107	[To avoid]
108	London Onion
111	Opinion

112	One day
113	Far away from
114	At first men were limited
114	The Prisoner
115	A fishbone fish a fefishbone
116	Pin
118	Die Gazelle zittert / The gazelle trembles

PROSES & PLAYS

121	The Onion
128	Kurt Schwitters to the Swiss Dadaist Arp. Blackberries (2)
129	A Quarter of the Feelings of Old Man Automato in His Ancestral Castle Atho
130	The Secret Drawer
134	Vexation Plays
135	Dramatic Sketch
136	Buckets
137	Augusta Bolte
165	Shepherd's Play
167	Shadow Play
173	Profane Words over the Eternal City
187	In the Middle of the World a House Stands
191	Two Choruses from *Above and Below*
197	The Family Plot
209	For Exhibition

POETICS

213	The Artists' Right to Self-Determination
215	From *Merz*
222	i

223　Consistent Poetry
225　What Is Madness?
226　Language
229　[What art is, you know . . .]
229　Grotesques and Satires
230　Numbers
231　typography and orthography: small letters
233　My Sonata in Primal Sounds
238　About me by myself
240　Stone upon stone is a building
241　Present Inter Noumenal
242　PIN

245　Chronology
249　Index of Titles
253　About the Translators

INTRODUCTION

THE MAN IN THE MYTH

> *he who walks with his house on*
> *his head is heaven he*
> *who walks with his house*
> *on his head is heaven he who walks*
> *with his house on his head*
> —Charles Olson, *Maximus II*

In the myth we see him as the Dada artist, founding his own movement in the world of art, lugging his art from place to place, victim of a politics and life he can't control. His center is Hannover, and the center's center is his house, inside of which he builds a column, a sculptural collage he calls "a monument to Dada" or, again, "cathedral of erotic misery." The column's growing, it's pushing through the ceiling, it spreads in all directions, grafting itself on adjacent rooms, breaking through walls and partitions, until it seems to fill the world. But it's not enough, the world is bigger. In 1936 he leaves it—his first flight from the terror of the total state—and makes his way to Norway, where he starts to build again. And again in 1940—now he's Olson's Man-With-His-House-On-His-Head—the darkness surrounds him and he sails for England, only to get thrown in prison there, a German alien in wartime. He stops writing, even stops speaking, German. Given some food, a place to sleep, and lots of garbage for his art (he says), he stays in prison for a year—then on release, out in the British countryside, starts building it again. At his death in 1947, the house in Hannover has been destroyed by bombs, the one in England stands unfinished. In 1951 the house in Norway disappears in flames.

THE MAN IN THE POEMS

My aim is the total Merz art work, which combines all genres into an artistic unity. First, I married off single genres. I pasted words and sentences together into poems in such a way that their rhythmic composition created a kind of drawing. The other way around, I pasted together pictures and drawings containing sentences that demand to be read. I drove nails into pictures in such a way that besides the pictorial effect a plastic relief effect arose. I did this in order to erase the boundaries between the arts. —Kurt Schwitters

Although Kurt Schwitters is increasingly recognized as one of the great visual artists of the twentieth century—a recognition reconfirmed in 1985 by a highly acclaimed retrospective at New York's Museum of Modern Art—his achievement as one of the major poets and theorists of Modernism has so far not received the same degree of attention, at least not in the English-speaking world. Art critics and museum curators, perhaps because of their own professional leanings, tend with few exceptions to consider his language-oriented work as a curious by-product of his art, or even as a minor phase of his early, Dada-associated career. While such an appraisal may be true for an artist and occasional writer like Picasso, in this case it is more than an unfortunate oversight—it is a major distortion of Schwitters' accomplishment, especially because he himself never saw his various art and literary activities according to some such hierarchical model. On the contrary, Schwitters' push was toward an ever greater integration and equivalence of the various facets of his artistic *oeuvre*. In this sense—in that extension of Dada experimentation that he personalized with the coined word Merz—his attempt "to erase the boundaries between the arts" resembles and predicts the work of such later artists as Cage, Oldenburg, and Kaprow, indeed of a significant portion of the "postmodern" generation.

Schwitters wrote prolifically throughout his life. His earliest poems date from his student days in pre-World War One Germany, his last writings from 1947, the year before his death in England. It is in his poetry, he tells us, that he made his initial breakthrough as an artist, and it is in the fusion of the poetry and painting that he made his entry into Merz. Besides the poetry, the boundaries of which he stretched as much if not more than any of his contemporaries, he wrote essays and manifestos, plays and fictions. Although most of his writing was in his native German, he also wrote in English and Norwegian (he renounced the German language during his exile in World War Two). The true extent of his written opus has only recently become apparent, thanks to the five volumes of his collected writings (*Das literarische Werk*) published by DuMont Verlag in Cologne.

Kurt Schwitters' continual inventiveness is revealed by even a cursory glance at his collected writings. He ranks squarely among the protean writers of the first part of the twentieth century, along with figures such as Apollinaire, Stein, Tzara, Marinetti, Pound, and so on. The professed sweep and aim of his poems (no contemporary poet worked with or developed more new forms and genres) are truly Poundian or even Wagnerian, though without Pound's or Wagner's mythohistorical ambitions or ideological strictures. Schwitters worked all his life toward a *Gesamtkunstwerk*, a total work of art, as an amalgamation of elements from all artistic genres assembled through the common synthesizing principle of radical collage. His famous Merzbau (Merz tower) was "an extraordinary architectural-sculptural column, or assemblage," as Lucy Lippard describes it, or Schwitters himself in a letter from 1946: "My Merz tower was not confined to a single room, but spread over the whole house.... Parts of it were in the adjoining rooms, on the balcony, in 2 rooms of the cellar, on the 2nd floor, in the attic." And again: "I am building an abstract sculpture into which people can go."

Schwitters also conceived but never brought into full play the idea of a Robert Wilson-like total theater, as what he called "the ultimate, total Merz work . . . , distinguished by the fusion of all factors [even people can be included] into a total work of art." While unable to put his ideas for the Merz stage into practice, Schwitters wrote tirelessly about how he imagined it to be, this final incarnation of his dream of art. Thus, in his 1920 essay "Merz":

The Merz stage knows only the fusion of all the parts into the total work. Materials for the stage set are all solid, liquid, and gaseous bodies such as white wall, man, barbed-wire fence, water stream, blue distance, light cone. Use surfaces that can become solid or dissolve into gossamer meshes, surfaces that can fold like curtains, shrink or expand. Let things turn on themselves and move; let lines broaden into surfaces. Parts will be inserted into the set while other parts will be removed. The materials for the score consist of all sounds and noises that can be created by violin, drum, trumpet, sewing machine, ticking clock, water stream, etcetera. The materials for the text are all experiences that excite the brain and the emotions. These materials are not to be used logically in their objective relationships, but only within the logic of the work of art. The more intensively the work of art destroys rational objective logic, the greater the possibilities of artistic form. Just as in poetry word is played off against word, so in this instance one will play off factor against factor, material against material.

But even in his smaller visual collages, words invaded the world of paint and form, not only as detritus from the commercial/banal worlds around him, but speaking to the issues of his time—signs of a democratizing politics and of a poetics of everyday life: "the search for an artistic complex in an artless world . . . and from that complex the creation of works of art through acts of framing." This highly conscious quest to use everyday objects and language shards— "banalities" he calls them—is foregrounded by Schwitters in a number of theoretical texts. In "Banalities (4)" he writes:

Not all banalities are totally dada, but every banality hides a load of dadaistic nonsense. I have merzed banalities, i.e., made works of art by juxtaposing and evaluating sentences that, taken by themselves, are banal. I am also conscious of the fact that not all the sentences I used are banalities. The reader has to decide for himself. For "there is an essence in us able to explode greenly" (Theodor Däubler). I do not dare to decide if "Lord, Lord, give me strength" is banal, given the quantity of explosive force stored in this sentence; it is probably expressionism. Lordy Lord, give me your Sturm! It is, to say the least, a direct order from a man who feels powerless and is essentially not different from me saying: "Mrs. Meier, give me two ounces of coffee!" At which Mrs. Meier is likely to explode greenly. And thus we have also managed to reduce expressionism to its simplest formula: "An exchange of spiritual goods," where the spirit consists of the fact that one cannot check the weight of the strength as easily as that of the coffee.

In all of these enterprises the relation between language and art is continuous and all-pervasive, and Schwitters is at all times both an artist and a poet.

Viewed in the narrower sense, Schwitters' poetry-as-such displays a similar sweep and inventiveness. It includes early expressionistic lyrics (the most radical of which—strongly influenced by the experimental expressionism of August Stramm—already move him toward his kind of asyntactical poetry) and their later, often hilarious, reworkings ("An Anna Blume" is the primary example); Dada and proto-Surrealist poems; and vocovisual experiments, often taking the shape of what would later be called sound texts and concrete poetry. While he is best known for the latter works (his "Ur Sonata" foremost here), his language experiments led him also into other areas of what he called "abstract poetry," where syntax was dissolved or transformed, isolating words or placing them in untried combinations, as an exploration of the problematics of referentiality and nonreferentiality in language:

Desire
And
Without
Have
Sing
Earthworm
   Strut
Lyric
Tradition
The beggar
   Of
Hollow
Green
Of about
Of abutments
The grass.

Of such works he writes: "In poetry, words are torn from their former context, dissociated, and, brought into a new artistic context, they become formal parts of the poem, nothing else." His central methods here, as with his best known paintings, are those of collage and assemblage, or, as he describes it: "[The poetry] is analogous to Merz painting in making use of given elements such as sentences cut out of newspapers or taken down from catalogues, posters, etc., with or without alteration." Along the same lines he remains as open to voices as to written words—attentive, as a Gertrude Stein would also be—to the sounds of fractured conversations, which he makes into the building blocks of early poems like "Profane Words over the Eternal City" or the more narratively structured "Flight" that marks the start of the 1940 journey toward his final exile.

In the grand scheme, too, Schwitters' Merz poetry may be seen to include prose works like "Murder Machine 43" or "The Onion," along the lines of what the American poet Ron Silliman, writing in the 1980s, called "the new sentence." There is also that in Schwitters which reminds us of work like the 1950s "cut-ups" and "fold-ins" of Brion Gysin and William Burroughs. Gysin, who came in fact from painting to writing, where work of this sort has had such little play, made the reasonable observation that "writing is fifty years behind painting." Yet, if Gysin's remark reflects on the late reception of earlier experimental poetry, it also points to the degree to which Schwitters' workings as a poet preceded or paralleled his workings as a painter.

In looking at those workings, then, it is impossible to keep a sharp division between the poetry and painting. The pursuit of diverse forms, Schwitters wrote, "was an artistic necessity for me . . . [and] the reason for it was not so much a desire for a widening of the scope of my work, but rather the endeavor to be an artist and not a specialist in one genre." The key term in either case was abstraction, not as a formal device but toward a recovery of the *spiritual* in art (Kandinsky's term) and as a reflection of, and comment on, the time in which he lived. In both instances he employed collage as a procedure by which to bring the world of non-art (= "life") into his frame; in both he sought for elementary forms (as letters, consonants and vowels, numbers, primal sounds) to act as building blocks for something older, newer. The intermingling was everywhere, inseparable. As John Elderfield describes it:

In Schwitters' case, the arts he practiced not only share a common structure, the principle of collage, but are interrelated and mixable. Painting and poetry come together in the pasted words and phrases of his collages; the ready-found phrases of the poems are joined in collage-like word-chains; the Dadaist and rubber-stamp drawings juxtapose literary and graphic forms in one structure, while the imagery of these drawings is also found in Schwitters' poems and prose, and in some of the early Dadaist sculptures as well. Schwitters emphasized the reciprocal relationship of his visual and literary work, saying he made poems that could be looked at as drawings, collages that could be partly read, and pictures that contained elements of collage, of poetry, and indeed of sculpture too.

Even the titles of his workings and paintings sometimes were, he said, "a poem about the picture."

But for all of his radical language experiments, Schwitters, during his most active period on native ground, was the author of what was possibly the best known and most popular German poem of the 1920s, "An Anna Blume"; and his almost equally popular "Ur Sonata," a wordless thirty-five-minute performance poem, is to sound poetry what Joyce's *Ulysses* is to the twentieth-century novel. If the success of "An Anna Blume"—"both a Dadaist poem . . . and a sentimentalized Expressionist one," as Elderfield describes it—came easily, the success of the "Ur Sonata" was more equivocal and depended in large measure on Schwitters' own personality and presence as a performer. This involved not only his performance tours with avant-garde colleagues like Theo van Doesburg and Raoul Hausmann, but appearances like the one described in almost mythic terms by the Dada artist and filmmaker Hans Richter, which took place in Potsdam in 1924 or 1925 in a private house and before an audience made up largely of the local gentry: retired generals and other people of rank from the old Prussian nobility:

Schwitters stood on the podium, drew himself up to his full six feet plus, and began to perform the Ursonate, complete with hisses, roars and crowings, before an audience who had no experience whatever of anything modern. At first they were completely baffled, but after a couple minutes the shock began to wear off. For another five minutes, protest was held in check by the respect due Frau Kiepenhauer's house. But this restraint served only to increase the inner tension. I watched delightedly as two generals in front of me pursed their lips as hard as they could to stop themselves laughing. Their faces, above their upright collars, turned first red, then slightly bluish. And then they lost control. They burst out laughing, and the whole audience, freed from the pressure that had been building up inside them, exploded in an orgy of laughter. The dignified old ladies, the stiff generals, shrieked with laughter, gasped for breath, slapped their thighs, choked themselves.

Kurtchen was not in the least bit put out by this. He turned up the volume of his enormous voice to Force Ten and simply swamped the storm of laughter in the audience, so that the latter seemed almost to be an accompaniment to the Ursonate. . . . The hurricane blew itself out as rapidly as it had arisen. Schwitters spoke the rest of his Ursonate without further interruption. The result was fantastic. The same generals, the same rich ladies, who had previously laughed until they cried, now came to Schwitters, again with tears in their eyes, almost stuttering with admiration and gratitude. Something had been opened up within them, something they had never expected to feel: a great joy.

There is no anonymous or absent author here, but a remarkable, self-defined, and often misunderstood artist.

THE MAN IN HIS TIMES

The goal is serious, the way humorous. Or sarcastic. Or a game. Everybody's life is wholly like that, when lived without external coercion. We play until death takes us away. — Kurt Schwitters, in 1946 letter to Christof Spengemann

Kurt Hermann Edward Karl Julius Schwitters was born on June 20, 1887, in Hannover, the son of middle-class parents, who owned and ran a highly successful *Modewarengeschäft* (fashion shop). They did well enough so that at forty his father could give up his business, buy five houses in Hannover, and live off the income. The family lived in one of these houses, Waldhausenstrasse 5, an important Schwitters address, for that is where the son would also live, where he would build his first Merzbau, and which he would reluctantly leave behind him when forced into exile in the 1930s. As Werner Schmalenbach points out, Schwitters had "no material worries until 1918," partly because of his parents' wealth and partly because he himself was working as a commercial artist. But he gave up that job during the German revolution of 1918, and owing to the spiraling inflation, his parents were no longer able to help him. From then on he lived on income received either through free-lance activities as a graphic designer or through whatever moneys he could generate through his art work and public performances. Much of his later traveling and long absences from his beloved Hannover were forced upon him in the search for a subsistence income for himself and his family.

After graduating from high school in 1908, Schwitters spent a year at the Kunstgewerbeschule (college of commercial arts and crafts) in Hannover. From 1909 to 1914 he studied at the College of Art in Dresden, following the rather traditional curriculum of art students, something of which he reminds us in his 1920 essay "Merz":

I studied the technique of painting with Bantzer, Kühl and Hegenbarth in Dresden. I painted the still life with Last Supper Chalice in Bantzer's studio. . . . I progressed from the most accurate possible imitation of nature with oil paint, brush, and canvas to the consistent transformation of exclusively artistic components in the Merz object, [so] that there is a continuous development from these naturalistic studies to the Merz abstractions.

War broke out in 1914, and the next year Schwitters married Helma Fischer, a distant cousin, and settled in the Waldhausenstrasse house. In 1917 he was called up for military service and quickly declared ineligible for active duty. After spending several months behind a desk—while doing everything in his dadaistic power to be kicked out—he was finally discharged. As he put it later: "During the war I fought on every front on Waterloo Square in Hannover, but never on the battlefield." In June 1917 he started work as an industrial designer in the Wülfel Ironworks, but gave up that position during the first days of the 1918 revolution, and went on to study architecture for two semesters. Of his work experience he wrote: "As soon as the great and glorious revolution broke out, I handed in my resignation and now live completely from my art." Schwitters' relation to the aborted German revolution, though initially jubilant, was tinged with both irony and sadness. In a 1930 autobiographical piece he wrote: "I do not care much for such revolutions; mankind needs to be ripe for them. It is as if the wind blew down unripe apples, what a waste! But thanks to it the whole con game which humans call war came to an end."

The end of the war in 1918 (his only child, Ernst, was also born that year) clearly marked a great sense of liberation for Schwitters, both on a personal and on an artistic level:

Only now did the great ferment begin for real. I felt free and needed to loudly proclaim my sense of jubilation in the face of the world. From a sense of thriftiness—ours was a very poor country then—I used whatever I could find for this purpose. One can also jubilate with the help of garbage, and that's what I did, gluing or nailing bits of it together.

This was the birth of what Schwitters would soon call Merz, deriving the name from a collaged fragment of the word *Kommerzbank*, or, as he also explained it, from the German verb *ausmerzen*, denoting a process of discarding or weeding out. In one of his many discussions of the word and concept he defined it as "my prayer for the victorious resolution of the war, for once again peace had won out over war. Everything was in ruins anyway, and something new had to be won from all these shards. That is Merz. I painted, nailed, glued, wrote, and experienced the world in Berlin." Although he had already been in contact with many German and foreign avant-garde artists during the war, his visits to Berlin ("the cheapest city in the world, which is why so many millions of interesting foreigners live there") put him in touch with a highly energetic and cosmopolitan art world.

But the center of his manifold activities—at least for another decade—remained Hannover, to which he soon returned. While this sense of place, of rootedness, goes much deeper than those who labeled it as a petty bourgeois deviation were able to perceive, during that most cosmopolitan decade of the century, it must have seemed odd to many a casual spectator or reader. (To others among the militant Berlin avant-garde it was taken as an out-and-out betrayal.) Rather than limiting Schwitters' art, however, this insistence brought both the art and the thinking *about* the art into areas of concern that were not explored in any depth until much later—in the "New American Poetry" of the 1950s and 1960s, for example, or, as far as the "banal" local materials of his art (both visual and vocal) were concerned, by certain aspects of pop art and performance. If, as the above quote makes clear, the choice of found (i.e., free) "garbage" for his art was at first based on historical necessity and monetary constraints, it is also obvious that it was a political choice, based on a deeply democratic view of art. As proof of this one need only think of Schwitters' use of similar found and banal materials in his language works, where the cost of the materials could hardly be at issue.

That Schwitters was well aware of what was going on in avant-garde art beyond Hannover is obvious if one looks closely at his virtually one-man movement and its close affinities with the Zurich and Berlin Dada groups, with Russian and Italian Futurists and Constructivists, and with Dutch poets and artists (Van Doesburg, Mondrian, et al.) connected with *De Stijl* . In Berlin he had met, among many others, the painter and poet Hans Arp, with whom he was to stay on very close terms all his life, and Raoul Hausmann, one of the central figures of Dada. He had also made contact with Herwarth Walden, a principal sponsor of Expressionism, who was to show Schwitters' art in his Sturm Gallery and print his writings in his magazine, *Sturm*, from 1919 on. Back in Hannover, Schwitters began to correspond with Tristan Tzara, which led to the publication of several of his poems in the last of the Zurich Dada publications, *Der Zeltweg*. These early postwar years were a creative whirlwind for Schwitters, whose daily life Hans Richter compares to "a living epic" and describes as follows:

Something dramatic was always happening. The Trojan war cannot have been as full of incident as one day in Schwitters' life. When he was not writing poetry, he was pasting up collages. When he was not pasting, he was building his column, washing his feet in the same water as his guinea pigs, warming his paste-pot in the bed, feeding the tortoise in the rarely used bathtub, declaiming, drawing, printing, cutting up magazines, entertaining his friends, publishing Merz, writing letters, loving, designing all Günther Wagner's printing and publicity material (for a regular fee), teaching academic drawing, painting really terrible portraits, which he loved, and which he then cut up and used piecemeal in abstract collages, assembling bits of broken furniture in MERZ pictures, shouting to Helmchen, his wife, to attend to Lehman [sic], his son, inviting his friends to very frugal luncheons . . . and in the midst of all this he never forgot, wherever he went, to pick up discarded rubbish and stow it in his pockets. All this he did with an instinctive alertness of spirit, an intensity, that never failed.

This intensity soon paid off. In 1919 the small avant-garde Hannover publisher Paul Steegemann brought out a collection of Schwitters' poetry and prose under the title *Anna Blume*, the success of which catapulted Schwitters to the forefront of not only the German but the international avant-garde. Better still, the poem "An Anna Blume" ("Anna Blossom Has Wheels") became an instant popular success, something few avant-garde works could lay a claim to.

The popularity of "Anna Blume" (Schwitters was, in this sense, more "successful" as a writer than as a painter) had its negative side as well. What it did was to fuel the antagonism from the more political Berlin Dadas, those like Richard Huelsenbeck and George Grosz who had reinterpreted Dada as the equivalent of "German bolshevism." The image they projected of Schwitters as an apolitical and bourgeois artist, both in background and in action, has remained a part of the Schwitters myth down to the present time. And yet the work itself—and his writings make this abundantly clear—was permeated like theirs by a sense of the social and political present. More than the democratization of his materials or his tentative exhilaration in the face of revolution to which we've already pointed, his selection of a specific content was as often as not referential to the crises and conflicts of his time. What was lacking of course was a recognizably doctrinaire position, but in that sense, as Schwitters clearly knew, he represented an avant-garde impulse toward what his Dada enemy, Huelsenbeck, had spoken of as "the liberation of the creative forces from the tutelage of the advocates of power."

In the distinction that he drew between his own form of Dada and that of Huelsenbeck and Grosz, Schwitters came out strongly on the side of art as a force inherently disruptive of the closed order and power of the nation state: "Merz stands for freedom from all fetters, for the sake of artistic creation." And again, with full awareness of the ironies involved: "Art is too precious to be misused as a tool; I prefer to distance myself from contemporary events. . . . But I am more deeply rooted in my time than the politicians who hover over the decade." In the anarchic laughter that resonates, both implicitly and explicitly, throughout Schwitters' writings and art, in the caustic humor of his performance work (so close in spirit to that of Till Eulenspiegel—that older, mythic trickster figure from Saxony, that is, from Schwitters' own homeground), we can detect a stance that is, in the final analysis, more profoundly radical than many of the overtly political writings of his contemporary detractors.

With some such faith in his ability to transform by example, Schwitters began in the early 1920s to engage in a series of travels and poetry readings that would make him known as a performer throughout Europe. In September 1921, he and his wife, Helma, traveled with Raoul Hausmann and Hanna Höch to Prague, where he heard Hausmann's poem "fmsbw" for the first time, a poem that would become the starting point for his own "Ur Sonata." (He would return to Prague in 1926 and 1928.) In September 1922, Schwitters, together with Tzara, the Van Doesburgs, László Moholy-Nagy, El Lissitzky, Hans Richter, and others, held Dada readings in Weimar, Jena, and Hannover. Later that fall he joined the Van Doesburgs and Vilmos Huszár in Holland for a series of readings and Dada events, a trip that was to last until the spring of 1923. Twice, too, he traveled to Paris—in 1927 and in 1936—where he met André Breton but spent most of his time with his close friend Arp. When at home in Hannover, he organized a Merz evening at least once a month, while giving innumerable readings elsewhere in Germany.

During this period Schwitters also published a magazine, *Merz*, twenty-four issues of which came out between 1923 and 1932. Besides being the main platform for Schwitters' own Merz works and poetics, the magazine published art works and writings by a wide variety of artists: Tzara, Georges Ribémont-Dessaignes, Moholy-Nagy, Theo Van Doesburg (under the pseudonym of I. K. Bonset), Man Ray, Francis Picabia, Picasso, and others. He continued to earn his living as a commercial artist, and this led him, like other artists of his time, to rethink many aspects of typography, an area in which he was stimulated by the aesthetics of his Bauhaus friends and collaborators. As the contents of his magazine clearly indicate, Schwitters was also deeply interested in architecture, publishing work by Gerrit Rietveld and Van Doesburg, Vladimir Tatlin, and Walter Gropius, while he himself wrote essays on architecture for the Dutch magazine *i 10*. The great synthesis of these activities was to be the Merz *Gesamtkunstwerk*—his concept of a total work of art—already discussed above. Unhappily he was never able to put his ideas for the Merz stage into practice.

This feverish activity of the 1920s began to ebb with the coming to power of the Nazi regime in 1933. Although Schwitters himself was not persecuted at first (there were no racial or activist political grounds for the Nazis to do so), his situation became more and more untenable. In 1937, the infamous *Entartete Kunst* (degenerate art) exhibition in Munich contained works by Schwitters, and soon all his paintings and collages were removed from display in German museums. Schwitters was aware that he was in imminent danger of being arrested, and in early 1937 he and his son, Ernst, left Germany for Norway—only a few days ahead of the Gestapo, which made several attempts to arrest him in his home.

He settled in Lysaker, a small town near Oslo, but spent most of the summer months in Molde on the island of Hjertøy, where he had rented an old smithy. In Lysaker, meanwhile, he started work on a new Merzbau. Helma visited him and Ernst for a few months every year until the beginning of the war, but otherwise remained in Hannover, managing the family affairs, and died there in 1945 without having seen her husband again. (She is presented later as the heroine Wilhelma in his 1946 anti-Nazi play *The Family Plot* [*Die Familiengruft*], in which his mother-in-law is cast as the Nazi anti-heroine Nora.) Life for Schwitters wasn't easy; he paid his way by painting portraits and landscapes, which he sold to hotels and tourists, but Norway had no truck with his avant-garde ideas. Although he remained in contact with his many international friends—at least until the war—

life in Norway was not as fulfilling as he would have liked it to be, and from all accounts he was extremely depressed during the first years of his exile. In 1939 he started to make plans to emigrate to the United States, but the outbreak of the war prevented this. When German troops occupied Norway in April 1940, he and his son fled north, barely a day ahead of the Gestapo. Ernst Schwitters describes the two-month-long flight as follows:

Despite the fateful difficulties, Kurt Schwitters never completely lost his warm humor, and the long days and weeks of our flight—by land and sea—through a strife-torn Norway—with a small sculpture of birchwood and a pocket knife in one of his pockets, and two white mice, temporarily housed in a cardboard box, in the other—have remained unforgettable. . . . The sculpture was finished during the flight. The white mice would pop up most unexpectedly and always in the most inappropriate circumstances, which, combined with Schwitters' decidedly German accent, soon gave rise to dark rumors of bacteriological warfare.

Schwitters' own description of the departure from Norway—a realistic extension of his workings with voice collage—appears in his 1940 poem "Flight."

When he finally reached England, Schwitters was detained as an enemy national and had to spend seventeen months in a prison camp before gaining his release. During his internment on the Isle of Man he managed to have a small studio set up and started to paint and sculpt again, even to organize a number of Merz evenings, complete with conferences and readings. In the fall of 1942 he was set free and moved to London, where he would reside until the war's end. Life even then remained extremely difficult, and although he did have several exhibitions—as well as the admiration of critics such as Roland Penrose and Herbert Read—he could gain neither support nor recognition from his art as such. In 1944 he suffered a minor stroke and was cared for thereafter by Edith Thomas, a nurse, who would also be his last companion. When Ernst Schwitters moved back to Norway in 1945, Schwitters and Edith Thomas, unable to make ends meet in London, moved to Ambleside in the Lake District. There Schwitters started work on his third and last Merzbau, which remained unfinished at his death in 1948.

THE MAN IN THE BOOK

The word Merz had no meaning when I found it. Now it has the meaning which I gave it. The meaning of the concept Merz changes with the change in insight of those who continue to work with it. — Kurt Schwitters

In bringing Schwitters into the present we were aware—increasingly—of how much his work resembled and impacted our own. There is clearly more than a single Schwitters moving through his writings, and we've tried accordingly to show some of his range, while acknowledging that his principal pull for us was in the area of the experimental and avant-garde viewed as the continuing struggle with a form and content. In this sense the work crescendos in the early Merz years, moves toward the more conventional and obvious in the 1930s, and enters into a new problematic and invigoration during his final exile. In those last years, too, he makes a remarkable shift to a quirky, collagist's use of English, not as a native language but as an instrument, a new material or pigment, so to speak, for that central work of assemblage in which he remained engaged.

In the initial volume of *Das literarische Werk* (Schwitters' "*lyrik*," or poetry-as-such), from which our own first section is largely drawn, Friedhelm Lach as editor offers an elaborate series of generic subsets: poems, poems from England, banalities, *schlager* (pop tunes) and songs, and concrete poetry (including sound texts). The subsequent volumes then take up—in the following order—the early and late prose, the plays and sketches, and the manifestos and critical writings. Since these categories seem to be Lach's rather than Schwitters', we have attempted, at least with the *lyrik* part, to show it as a single, chronologically ordered unit, in particular not to separate the German from the English or the concrete and sound works from the "poems that look like poems." For the rest, however, we've succumbed to the temptation to offer proses (our own term) and performance works (including theater) as a second set and manifestos/poetics as a third. Still, the overlap throughout is unmistakable, and the reader can feel free to question or to change the ordering as she or he sees fit. Is "The Onion," for example—subtitled "Merzpoem 8"—a poem or a kind of prose work/fiction? (The answer of course is "both" or "neither.") And yet the subset of "proses and performance pieces" (even with the major sound poems otherwise disposed) seems workable enough to us, and the final subset ("poetics") is clearly essential for our presentation of Schwitters as a thinking and thoroughly self-conscious artist.

We have also been determined to include *complete* major works like "Augusta Bolte" and "Ur Sonata," to make the latter text available to the American reader who might want to have a go at it in his or her own voice. By contrast, we have only provided an excerpt from Schwitters' long play *Above and Below,* from a sense perhaps that its inherent *expressionismus* would, when translated, have little to say to a reader in the 1990s. Some of our other offerings also have, we feel, a largely token quality—the presentation, for example, of only a few of the collaged and word-filled paintings, which should, in an ideal viewing of Schwitters' language works, assume a much more central place. In so doing, however, we have insisted that these works appear in color—remembering, as with later concrete poetry (some of the poems of Emmett Williams or of Ian Hamilton Finlay come to mind), that color is also an element at the service of those poets who would care to use it.

With Schwitters' work, too, unlike that of other foreign writers, it seems obvious that a significant part of the output would necessarily appear without translation: the poems written in English, the visual and many of the concrete works, the sound poems. With those inclusions, then, that show no translator's credits in the text, it should be noted that we are only functioning as editors and selectors. With the German on the other hand, we also enter as translators, but here too—as in Schwitters' own English version of "Anna Blume"—Schwitters stays ahead of us, provides us through these and through his English poems a clue to those moves of language—melopoeia, logopoeia—by which to bring him into English. Thus it's Schwitters who gives the green light for our extensive use of second-person thou's, sometimes correctly grammatical, sometimes linked to first-person verbs. And it's Schwitters who sets a model for moving among the banalities of everyday speech, of newspaper prose, and of high-flown lyrical diction. Some of this points also to those characteristics of his poetry—derived from Expressionism or of his own invention—in which parts of speech, say, are transposed, the nouns becoming verbs, the verbs (less often) nouns. In written

German, the use of caps for nouns, lower case for verbs, alerts the reader to such transpositions, while the issue in English is left up in the air or is partly resolved—also with a hint from Schwitters—by the use of the auxiliary verbs "do" and "does." As poets as much as translators, we find ourselves attending to such details, while trying to remain open and innovative on our own, playing in and out between his meanings. In so doing we hope to have resisted the final temptation of the translator, that of saying more than Schwitters did, of clearing up what Schwitters meant to leave ambiguous, abstract—a pathway too rigorous to follow or to reconstruct.

For much the same reason, we have omitted almost all footnotes from this volume (the few we have added are enclosed in brackets), although the work is full of references to persons and events from Schwitters' time that may seem obscure in our own. We trust that the reader will recognize in Schwitters' poetry of displacements and juxtapositions—of collage in short—an array of contemporary references in which the types, if not their more precise particulars, are clear enough in context. Some names of artists or writers (Chagall, Arp, Marc, Apollinaire) have largely remained familiar; others (Expressionists like Walden, Johannes Molzahn, Rudolf Blümner, Rudolf Bauer; Dadaists like Walter Serner, Walter Mehring; premodernists like Giovanni Segantini, Arnold Böcklin) have largely not. Contemporary political figures (Matthias Erzberger or Gustav Noske, say) can still barely be discerned as such, while fictional creations (Anna Blume or Augusta Bolte, Elvis Broomsticker or Franz Müller) are as true to life (or not) as when he made them. Strikes and political movements may appear—as they did then—as headlines and sentences ripped from the daily news; and the daily news itself (as *Deutsche Tageszeitung*) will reveal whatever meaning it still holds in the assemblage as a whole. Schwitters' poetry is rarely overwhelmed by such details, and the clue to dealing with them is very much as with allusions or images that turn up in his otherwise "abstract" paintings. His is an art, then, in which "things" come through (or don't) at much their own pace, and we would not want to take away from the quality of the barely overheard and barely understood by an intrusion of ourselves as unwanted guides and docents.

Finally, while we were reading, translating, and assembling Schwitters, we came again to realize how alive his work remains for poets writing here and now.

His idea of a work of art—a Merz work—that would change in time with the perceptions of those who might embrace it, plays itself out in such an enterprise as Jackson Mac Low's "*Merzgedichte* in Memoriam Kurt Schwitters," which has continued to appear during the time of our working. There have been others as well, including one of the present editors, who have sought in their own poetry to address and celebrate the "dada strain" in Schwitters' work. The latent power of that work in the present is perhaps best exemplified by an event recorded by the British jazz musician George Melly. Late one night he decided to take a break between two sets in a London jazz club. As he stepped into the alleyway behind the club for a breath of fresh air, a menacing figure suddenly loomed before him, wielding a knife and demanding his money. Melly's spontaneous response was to start reciting the "Ur Sonata" at the top of his voice—which baffled and scared his assailant so much that he dropped the knife and ran. No matter how apocryphal this anecdote may turn out to be, Schwitters would have loved it, for, as he put it in one of the last poems he wrote: "The gazelle trembles, / As the lions roar. / The hyena shambles, / But ART GIVES MORE."

Jerome Rothenberg & Pierre Joris   *Encinitas, 1991/1992*

EDITORS' NOTE

In compiling these writings—our designation *pppppp* derived from a Schwitters poem and its serendipitous relation to the works at hand—we have drawn throughout from the five-volume edition of *Das literarische Werk*, edited by Friedhelm Lach and published by DuMont Verlag in Cologne: volume 1, *Lyrik*, 1973; volume 2, *Prosa 1918–1930*, 1974; volume 3, *Prosa 1931–1948*, 1975; volume 4, *Schauspiele und Szenen*, 1977; volume 5, *Manifeste und kritische Prosa*, 1981. A number of other books have also proven of the greatest use, notably the two principal monographs on Schwitters, John Elderfield's *Kurt Schwitters* (Thames & Hudson, 1985) and Werner Schmalenbach's *Kurt Schwitters* (Prestel Verlag,

1984), to which we would add Michael Erlhoff's *Kurt Schwitters Almanach* (Postskriptum Verlag, 1982), the 1972 Schwitters issue of *Text + Kritik*, and such old standbys as Hans Richter's *Dada: Art and Anti-Art* and Robert Motherwell's *Dada Painters and Poets*. We are also immeasurably grateful to Larry Venuti, who with Toby Olson initiated this project for Temple University Press and who has given us the greatest possible encouragement and assistance in carrying it forward.

Translated works in these pages are identified by the initials JR, PJ, and KS. Those works not so identified were originally composed in English by Kurt Schwitters or were not in need of translation.

The editors would like to thank the following journals where some of the translations in this volume first appeared: *Bombay Gin* (Boulder, Colorado), "High Fashion Furs," "Wound roses roses bleed"; *Boulevard* (Philadelphia), "Flight"; *Conjunctions* (New York), "Analysis," "Four Bear Songs," "[1 7 10]," "The World"; *Grand Street* (New York), "The Onion"; Morning Star Publications (U.K.), "For Franz Marc," "The gazelle trembles," "Indecent i-Poem," "Legborders," "Light & Low," "Waggling"; *Scarlet* (New York), "Chinese Banalities"; *Sulfur* (Ypsilanti, Michigan), "Desire," "Execution," "A Flower Like a Raven," "From the Back & from the Front to Start," "Green Child," "Ice Clocks," "Murder Machine 43," "Repose," " 'Thou' "; *Talisman* (Hoboken, New Jersey), "She Dolls with Dollies"; and *TO: A Journal of Poetry, Prose and the Visual Arts* (Narberth, Pennsylvania), "The Bahnhof," "Consistent Poetry," "Evening," "The Hand," "Ideas for Poems," "Nights," "On a Drawing by Marc Chagall," "Short Biography," "What is Madness?"

POEMS & PERFORMANCE PIECES

1914–1918   **The World**
             Poem 2

             Houses are falling, skies caving in.
             Trees arise vast over trees.
             It is sky that greens into redness,
             Silvery fishes that swim through the air,
             Do not burn themselves out,
             Though they're ever so inward.
             In eternal silver the mornings do shine.
             Illusion swells up, flaunts it over the sky.
             Millions of silvery fish shake and quake in its vastness.
             But they don't singe their silvery wings.
             Soft bloweth the air from their silvery wingbeats.
             It is people who flaunt it— —
             Souls who kneel down— — —
             Vast does grow the illusion over that vastness.

             JR

1917   **Unstupid**

             So hear glant scream pained Morea
             Mamauer gleam dislarned thou I sing
             Shrill glowteth glant équalte fine
             Like wheel axles scream to scream
             Embers paineth bodyhot dislarned shine
             O hear! I dislarneth painèd pains.
                  Seeyoo Sibeelee splashes the moon
                  O see you, o sing along;
                  Libeelee goldens Glotea.
             But Paain Dream throttles my sing.

             PJ

1917–1918　　**Nights**
　　　　　　　Poem 7

　　　　　　　Heartfelt nights
　　　　　　　Embers anguish
　　　　　　　Shakes ember bliss
　　　　　　　Painful conjuncts
　　　　　　　Boiling rutty spends nights
　　　　　　　Whips fire firebolt
　　　　　　　Twitching salaciousness
　　　　　　　O could I but launder this fishy
　　　　　　　An inside shies shyly
　　　　　　　Shakes and unjuncts
　　　　　　　Lusts salaciously
　　　　　　　Tangy
　　　　　　　Thou
　　　　　　　O thou bride smell
　　　　　　　Roses glisten in gardens
　　　　　　　Fish spurs slimly in whipair
　　　　　　　Blemish knee
　　　　　　　Surfs breakers bliss
　　　　　　　If this fishy could fly
　　　　　　　I surge up
　　　　　　　Innerjoying
　　　　　　　Whips silently fervor
　　　　　　　Spills over shrilly
　　　　　　　Kneels dewropes on fishy
　　　　　　　His little leg slips
　　　　　　　Little white legs has the fishy
　　　　　　　Big white eyes has the death
　　　　　　　Firm does whip heartfelt night
　　　　　　　I
　　　　　　　Surge apart
　　　　　　　Does bleach it weary
　　　　　　　Does blue anguish sun

　　　　　　　J R

1917–1918   **"Thou"**

    My sing is void.
    Scream gapes,
    Scream swells up,
    Roars gapes swells.
    I bitter thou.
    I bitter thine breath.
    I sing thy eyes.
    Thy stride yearns my eyes.
    Thy blab my ear yearns.
    I lust the sniff of hours.
    Thou art my yearn
    Thou art thy stride, thy eyes, thy prayers.
    Thy laughing prays,
    Thy blab prays,
    Thy eye prays.
    My yearning fars thine pray cry.
    I
    Far thou

    JR

circa 1918   **Legborders**

    Borders
    Borders
    Borders
    A leg
    A
    leg
    Dig
    Dig
    A leg

    JR

circa 1918

Green Child
Poem 1

Enjailed air steeps.
The murder overdomes blood.
If only I could shard these walls!
Wall lechers us.
O this glow of the embracing wall!
Jail unifies—
Blood jails—
Blood steeps—
Giant-size blood overdomes.
Run—
Flee—
Fear—
Blood steeps—
Green.
Shot—
Who shoots?—
Blood?
Sulfur—
Feet overtrip—
Legs overrush—
Blood—
Fear—
Chase—
Fly—
Yell—
Blood grins yellow—bright—yellow—
Yellowgreen
Brightyellowgreen—
Sulfuryellowgreen—
Brightsulfuryellowgreen—
Blood grins brightsulfuryellowgreen.
If only I could wash the green blood!
Blood wash—
Bathe blood—
Blood bathe.

O thou rapturous white blood of my bride!
Greenblood steeps—
Yells—
Yawps?—
Brights—
Be silent yellowgreen blood!
Sulfur burns green!
I—
Run—
Yell—
I carry my pain in hands—
Like a child—
There, there, don't cry!
Dear, green, child!
Remember I'm your mother!
Dear child—
Green—
Is child crying?
Sulfuryellow child, how firered Thou art!
Red—
Blood—
Sulfuryellow—
Green—
Steeps damnation—
Chase—
Yell—
Torture—
Crazy is the hunt!
Happiness?
Thou happiness!
Thou I love!
Thou—
White blood, Thou!
But there steeps!
Sulfuryellow, green—
Disgusting green child!
We run,
On my arm.

Hold tight!
The walls hold tight!
We run walls—
Walls hold tight—
They leave you to me—
Thou and I—
Green child—
Thou and I—
Walls loom—
Blood steeps green.
Walls hold tight—
Yellowish understanding—
Darkred, breasting—
They want to take thee!—
No!
Only lech—
Give back—
Bloodred back—
Green child, how thou does look bloodred!
Outside black dogs fly.
Walls loom—
Walls hold tight—
I await—
Green child!
Blessed thy gaze!
Black dogs fly about the walls—
Green child,
You're mine!
Black dogs,
Fly us away!

PJ

circa 1918   **Wound roses roses bleed**
Poem 23

        Wound roses roses bleed
        Wound colossus wound wound
        Roses languish languish roses
        Torrid wound torrid torrid
        Languish roses languish languish
        Wound torrid wound wound
        Roses torrid torrid roses
        Embers trickle trickle ember
        Embers trickle trickle ember
        Bleed roses wound torrid
        Languish wounds rose blood
        Night languish roses night
        Night wound blood blood
        Night bleed night
        Blood night blood
        Blood bleeds
        Blood

        Silversound
        Wildwoodwondrous silversound
        Wildwoodsoothing silversound

        Silence trickle blood

        JR

circa 1918   **Light & Low**

Rollers
Rollers
Rollers
Lightly forgetting whipsaws whipsaws
And dipping
Lightly
Whipsaws
Forget
The dipsaws.

JR

1918–1920   **Cnudgel**
              Poem 46

              Stringthread becreeping earthworm.
              Berotted houses green up mountains tumble thighs spread
                 over thighs
              And cnudgel snails do slime up clumps.
              And towers flour houses.
              Skydome elevator ninehundredsixtyone.
              Fights down below below.
              People do spruce up entrails.
              Clamp nervelines wire weird staples.
              Rooftops flour houses over crust.
              Houses sharpeyed vertically implanted.
              Fogs to heave unborn new clumps.
              Streets slimedup deleafd.
              Becreeping roof.
              Besliming.
              Streakening.
              Dark boxes.
              Spaces.
              Boxes.
              Boxes.

              JR

circa 1919   **Madd Madd World**

I
Thou
He she it
We ye they,
A graveyard,
Living troutsauce overloud.
I over thou
Overloud
Troutgraveyard over
He thou troutfish
Lightly living
Thou!
A graveyard overlight
We live
We
Trout live graveyard
Living trout plays
  We play life
  I play thou,
    Lightly
  Do we play?
  Do we live?
    We
    Ye
   They

JR

circa 1919   **He She It**

Und
Hound
Tak
Pack
Caracts
Thouroundthou
Theeinthee
God help thou.
Live
Run
Endeavor
Forgive
Give
Theeinthee
Tak
Pack
Thouroundthou
You

PJ

1919   **Simultaneous Poem**
kaa   gee   dee

kaa gee dee	takepak	tapekek
katedraale	take	tape
draale	takepak	kek kek
kaa tee dee	takepak	tapekek
kateedraale	take	tape
draale	takepak	kek kek

| (all:) | oowenduumiir |

kaa tee dee	diimaan	tapekek
kateedraale	diimaan	tape
draale	diimaan	kek kek

| didiimaan | ------ | didiimaan |

| | diimaan | |

| (all:) | aawanduumiir |

1919   **Repose**

A little white cloud drops down from me.
In the valley I lie under lilies and call.
The breath from her hand shakes in the wind.
A big black cloud drops into the pot.
That the hangman's apprentice may bake it,
that it may be changed to ashes
and die.

JR

circa 1919   **An Anna Blume**

Oh Du, Geliebte meiner 27 Sinne, ich liebe Dir!
Du, Deiner, Dich Dir, ich Dir, Du mir,————wir?
Das gehört beiläufig nicht hierher!

Wer bist Du, ungezähltes Frauenzimmer, Du bist, bist Du?
Die Leute sagen, Du wärest.
Laß sie sagen, sie wissen nicht, wie der Kirchturm steht.

Du trägst den Hut auf Deinen Füßen und wanderst auf die Hände,
Auf den Händen wanderst Du.

Halloh, Deine roten Kleider, in weiße Falten zersägt,
Rot liebe ich Anna Blume, rot liebe ich Dir.
Du, Deiner, Dich Dir, ich Dir, Du mir,————wir?
Das gehört beiläufig in die kalte Glut!
Anna Blume, rote Anna Blume, wie sagen die Leute?

Preisfrage:

    1.) Anna Blume hat ein Vogel,
    2.) Anna Blume ist rot.
    3.) Welche Farbe hat der Vogel.

Blau ist die Farbe Deines gelben Haares,
Rot ist die Farbe deines grünen Vogels.
Du schlichtes Mädchen im Alltagskleid,
Du liebes grünes Tier, ich liebe Dir!
Du Deiner Dich Dir, ich Dir, Du mir,————wir!
Das gehört beiläufig in die———Glutenkiste.

Anna Blume, Anna, A————N————N————A!
Ich träufle Deinen Namen.
Dein Name tropft wie weiches Rindertalg.
Weißt Du es Anna, weißt Du es schon,
Man kann Dich auch von hinten lesen.
Und Du, Du Herrlichste von allen,

Du bist von hinten, wie von vorne:
A——————N——————N——————A.
Rindertalg träufelt STREICHELN über meinen Rücken.
Anna Blume,
Du tropfes Tier,
Ich———————liebe———————Dir!

1942   **Anna Blossom Has Wheels**

O Thou, beloved of my twenty seven senses,
I love thine!
Thou thee thee thine, I thine, thou mine.—we?
That belongs (by the side) not here!
Who art Thou, uncounted woman?
Thou art—art Thou?—
People say, Thou werst,—
Let them say, they don't know, how the churchtower stands.
You wearest your head on your feet and wanderst on your hands,
On thy hands wanderst Thou.
Hallo thy red dress, clashed in white folds,
Red I love Anna Blossom, red I love Thine!
Thou Thee Thee Thine, I Thine, Thou mine,—we?
That belongs (by the side) in the cold glow.
Red Blossom, red Anna Blossom, how say the people?
    Price question:
    1. Anna Blossom has wheels.
    2. Anna Blossom is red.
    3. what colours are the wheels?
Blue is the colour of thy yellow hair.
Red is the whirl of thy green wheels.
Thou simple maiden in everyday-dress,
Thou dear green animal,
I love Thine!
Thou Thee Thee Thine, I Thine, Thou mine—we?
That belongs (by the side) in the glow box.
Anna Blossom,

Anna,
A—N—N—A
I trickle your name.
Thy name drops like soft tallow.
Does thou know it, Anna,
Does thou allready know it?
One can also read thee from behind,
And thou, thou most glorious of all,
Thou art from the back, as from the front:
A—N—N—A
Tallow trickles to strike over my back.
Anna Blossom,
Thou drippes animal,
I
Love
Thine!

KS

circa 1919   **Call It Killing You Off**

Anna Blossom is the feeling just before and after bed
Anna Blossom is the woman there beside you
Anna Blossom is the only kind of love you still can do
Anna Blossom is truly you
To kill Anna Blossom means to kill you off too
Have you ever been offed in your whole life?
To kill off Anna Blossom means to off you too
Would you be willing to just let them off and kill you?
No! Kill Anna Blossom, the feeling just before going to bed
Kill Anna Blossom the woman there beside you
To kill Anna Blossom is the only offing you still can do
If you wouldn't be, Merz help you, a person who can't do it
    through and through

JR

circa 1919   **The Bahnhof**

They propped a ladder up against the sun
Sun being black
And flour mills flowering
Millions of people arching alarmbells
As hearts start emerging
Hearts start erupting
An arrow's too hearty for hearts
Hearts are arrowing
Sun's arrows hearting the flour mills
Wild lusts are raging
Thou thy thee thine
Thou thine thee thy.

JR

circa 1919   **Execution**
Merzpoem 9

Someone demanded Anna Blossom's execution. Execution triggers crucifixion. Crucifying Anna Blossom executes you all. Ring glows the knife gun turrets do trigger knives do swing. Ring glows the knife onto your headless heads. Ring to surge corpses headless frenzy, frenzy.
Humans! Humans brain humans. You humans with a human brain. (But really!) People are so wise, so Anna Blossom has a bird's brain. O Thou, beloved of my twenty seven senses, A—N—N—A, thou from the back as from, she that I love, thou thine thy thee, this may not be. Gardens do gobble world kiss. Gardens do blossom hands, meadows do dwell at teepees, sky wilts thread, and autumn cables times. But thou, thou noblest, thou greenest bird. Thou satiates to tint a knife the pastures. Does earth wilt? Do humans wander and must die? The crazy steel raised high sparkles thine limbs. Death inward hard whips inward door wine. Only now die, o thou wise one. Thou greens the human brain.

Thou greens to tremble human brains. Thou dies, I die a human, Anna Blossom does live worlds. O thou, beloved, thou greens life thou wiltest leaf.
Does thread wilt humans?
Poor old legs drop limbs.
Anna Blossom greens the wilt.

JR

1919   **To Johannes Molzahn**
Poem 37

Circle Worlds Thou.
Thou circles Worlds.
Thou overcometh chirping Apyl, of the waters the machine.
Worlds hurl Space.
You hurl worlds space.
Worlds turn the new machine for thee.
Thee.
Thou, thine the new machine Space.
And axles break eternity.
The work, to which we, us heirs, thou.

PJ

1919   **Herwarth Walden**

Thou sun!
Thy breath a dumbdumb door
Pant, pant last maws
Cats paws
Thou sun!
Thy breath what warmth
Dumb, dumb
Thy breath such joys
Thou sun!
Starwheels squeal dumbdumb doors
What joys.
(All young wheels strictly barred)

JR

1919   **Portrait of Herwarth Walden**

Glide stillscape roading roads.
The cigarette lips gold.
The stem of the cigarette wires stem.
A Tee the hand, and notes do ram roads, roads.
And roads orbit, hand the hands soft to the wheels.
Orbit stillscape roads orbit hand.
Roading sonorous roads.
Soft cigarette soften hair goal.
The goal, the goal.
And roads, roads, roads.
The silk silks cotton wool a hand the hand.

PJ

1919   **Portrait of Nell Walden**

Mutterfly flying silverchains,
Bloommouth blooms blond eyes blue.
Smile jewels fingertips.
And silverthreads spin arrows.
The lips send arrows question eyes.
And arrows net soft round edges.
Alluvia rounds fall veil, and the eye fars the sore question.

PJ

1919   **Portrait of Christof Spengemann**

Beansugar, beansugar.
Abrade eyes, thine soul.
Further ahead!
The ur-magnet abrades soul blue and green.
Struggles abraded soul eyes rope.
The way flies further ahead.
The way flies further ahead of the sugarbean.
And ahead and ahead unendingly eyes do bang.
The soul?
Girls sling thick lips velvetward.
But further, further, further ahead and ahead!

PJ

1919

Portrait of Rudolf Blümner
Poem 30

Of the voice burns the head acrossed the legs.
Grossed arms pained lurch bang for bang.
Usbeaming eatzing crawlie quake drizz.
And bang for bang.
Acrossed the bang disscorch shred strammish gush.
And bang for bang.
And bang for bang.
Cross arms leg gush the chair.
The chair's a screw, bracketwinding stramm.
And bang for bang of voice beheads.
The legs screw arms throttling letz.

PJ

1919

Portrait of Rudolf Bauer

Crack whirlyfishes whamblam boffo lilybone.
Couldya, wouldya know?
Wild soften hot cold, rosy, rosy.
Couldya rosy, wouldya know?
Blam boffo, lilyrose rosy bone.
Couldya wouldya want a rolling pin?
Bones crackle lilies rolling whirly rosy bones.
But hate you must find yellow rosy flame be found
Boffo must be couldya wouldya want?
Crackle whirlyfishes first it lets itself be twirled around.

JR

1919 **Mary the Red**

To singe to question thy blue tresses.
(Against the resolutions of the Majority Socialists.)
For thou'rt this bond.
Confusion noggins slaver loony.
Loony form.
Thou bloomest big eyes question questions.
Twelve o'clock all clocks do clock.

JR / PJ

1919 **To Maria**

Your neck strangles claw eyes
Moon fold traps do dream dreams the dream
In whirl your spray lamentations give aroma
You gave the band
Maria, you entower
Maria blows ruined deep dreams dream.

PJ

1919

On a Drawing by Marc Chagall
Poem 28

Playing card lyres fish, the head in the window.
The animal head lusts the bottle.
Athwart the bouncing mouth.
The headless man.
Hand wags sour knives.
Playing card fish squander dumpling bottle.
And a table drawer.
Too dumb.
And souly rounds the knob at table.
Fish pushes table, stomach sickens swordswipes.
Drunkard's stem dumbly does eye the doleful beast,
The eyes much lust the bottle's aromatics.

PJ/JR

Marc Chagall, *Der Trinker* (*The Drinker*), 1913. Pen, brush and ink, 8¼ x 11⅜ in. (21 x 29 cm.). © 1991 ARS, New York/ADAGP

1919   **A Flower Like a Raven**

A splashy "13" mirrored on the moon.
Flashy moon upon which tears did fall.
So ducky was the mouse.
Tears mirrored wave wave milded grief.
O were I but a wave!
A wave held tight at either end.
A wave descending upward.
A wave beached on the beach.
In the belltower clocks are boiling.
O could I but stretch the clock out on a wheel!
Its clockwork is a shining dew within.
Its rifts calmed by my soul.
A timid dewrope.
Blood grows an inner hand.
And pulses flow by millions.
Road enstarring
flowers.

JR

1919   **Private Gentlemen, Attention Please!**
Poem 29

Stealing is prohibited here, the occupant is a member of the civil defense. The power formation of a situation is in the grasping, as Noske proves. Today Ann received the following in Weimar: From the National Assembly of Piecemeal. As first formation of a serious situation weapons poisoned all. For he, who her, who here hear da da, goldens Glotea. (Dissolution of the family fathers.)

PJ

1919   **Decay's Way**

    Also this climbing around under the name "the" isn't
        unpleasant.
    The clock ungreens the creases, now does it preen in silk.
    Trumpets do climb up Anna Blossom elephant. (Radioactive.)
    The seats with the backs are the expensive seats.
    Thou.
    This great procedure that I also can't withhold from thee.
    The thou, there thou, this them.
    N.B. Anna Blossom and Arnold Böcklin have the same initials
        in their names: A. B.

    JR

1919   **Wheelers Dealers**

    Block elegantly licketh. (Ludolf, Mia.)
    Free Democrats do slug it out.
    Block infiltrate the state. (Anna Blossom hanging tough.)
    The state.
    Extasis putsches glory. (Holy hegemony in peril.) Potash.
    Foment a new strike. (Foment a new strike.)
    (Civic praise, peaceful days.)
    Erzberger namely.
    Lie quiet Erzberger! (Peaceful days.) — You fossild old farts.
    Under hands wheelers dealers macadamd (state-run
        bolshevists in England.)
    Here the move to majority views may account for
    the blocks to repressing mass cattle. (I love
    thou.) In Germany putsch anchor blooms a
    new strike. (Anna Blossom hangs soft.)
    Anna Blossom hangs tough. (Bittersalty.)
    The stirrersup stagger steal serpents. (On lease.)

    JR

1919   **Evening**
        Poem 25

        Glow caresses soft worlds kiss
        Whistle Sun Thread Sun (Zeppelin)
        I Thread Sun glimmerglare
        And glimmerglows softens world.

        PJ

1919   **Waggling**
        Poem 48

        Waggling.
        Earthworm.
        Fish.
        O'clock.
        The cow.
        The forest is leafing its leaves.
        A drop of asphalt in the snow.
        Cri, cri, cri, cri, cri.
        A wise man bursts without his perks.

        JR

1919   **From the Back & from the Front to Start**

    Labor volunteers.
    Sabotage   *strike*   hand grenades.
    Strike upheaves man.
    Teeth bark forth teeth.
    Infringements strike dismissals.
    Bark—bark—bark—bang—Fear culminates silverstrings.
    Drips stone on stone.
    The upper echelons!
    The upper echelons!
    Hand grenades fly by themselves. But you be endlessly cool-headed. Streetcars go both from the back & the front. Who rides on tourist buses? Easy—easy—you people all stand up—in line!—Head under foot: that's what I mean by a strike! Once & for all the tip money bends—it bends—the streetcars bent out of shape are gaping all over. Crooked hours. Hand back that young herring. But the upper echelons must act (this one walks on his hands 21/31) & must hold firm in the face of this illegal strike by a disgruntled & inefficient professional class (*German Daily News*), & especially here where its present behavior, not without effect on the upcoming strikes in Berlin and the rest of the Reich, cranks out head laughs. Lootings rob riots. (I say the opposite, viz., only not always.)
    The upper echelons!
    The upper echelons!
    The upper echelons & very.
    Culminates silverstrings stone on stone.
    Drips fear expulsions bang.
    Sabotage   *strike*   infringments.
    Drips silverstrings fear.
    Provisionally there exists no prospect to bring the thing together, the situation has no board of supervisors. (That our lovely plattdeutsch never be forgotten!) And an absolutely binding heat to strike your momma's feet. Four thousand, forty thousand cheap, this got a long ways still to go.—The Jews—the Jews!

    JR

1919   **Murder Machine 43**

Greetings, 260 thousand ccm.
I thine,
thou mine,
we me.
And sun unboundedness stars brighten up.
Sorrow sorrows dew.
O woe you me!
Official notices:
5000 marks reward!
A box is lopsided, forthwith your box.
There's no more ownership, it's only
communism that's hung up on ownership.
I am wilting the wicker, because no more wicker.
I am skimming the clock, because no more clock.
1, 2, 3, 4, 5, 6, seven.
Sunday is greening the warmth.
And the elephant.
Ah the fat elephant.

Should several persons post a claim for this reward, we reserve all rights to distribution with no recourse under law.
                    The Magistrate
            of this right royal seat and capital
                    I. V. Weber
One hour is black, how many lives love striving, since the cat does dance mosquitos squiggle rope black ink does silver dangle earthworm. Soda, soda, plenty soda in the corpse. But hark, 5000 marks reward! Visual artists strictly kept outside. First let them learn the rules most primitive of art. No schools no more, just factories. Art ground out in art factories. Here every artist gets a cubicle, the cubicles are furnished with straitjackets (to protect the public). Machines grind gyrate wheel brains. With which to set it off. I will, I will! Grabs giants bulge out overloud: I must? No, nobody must must. The artist wills, wills something: technique, morality, ideas, cathedrals, viz.: a program. 5000 marks for this lopsided box! Okay, we'll grind you out an earth-

worm palette a tricornered Segantini. (De mortuis nil, nisi bene.) Wicker to blitz filmy thatch. Oh what a program! I do stiffen wicker, pain does bang on doors. Because your thighs do bubble.

The key.

The key's lost. (I. V. Weber) 5000 marks reward against the author of most honored city manager, I wilt wind's leaf.

1, 2, 1, 2, 1, 2, 1.

Here died the owner of the Eagle Pharmacy. Overcome by his death that day was Senator Willy Kyland. For relief from shortages of fuel, the workers and soldiers council, playing with its urban bones, lost two good fingers on its right hand. The notary was torn asunder. This is something no good German would have wanted. We must protect our Fatherland against the worst! It is the duty of all Germans! Up up and join the ranks! Defend the National Assembly! Show there are still true German men amongst us! We have no weapons any longer. This is Expressionism.

Brothers in the Reich!

Millions of people work 24 hours a day, me too. It isn't good for a writer to have too many fans. Only marsh plants don't suffer from excessive moisture. It isn't good for a writer to have too many fans. We wind garlands round the geese we whimper rags, bones, iron. Rabbit skins bone legs. Diapers go crazy. Rabbit, o my little rabbit, thou!

Moving vans tie eyes up steam up flowers.

Lump lump lump.

Moving vans grin graybeards rotate appleboats.

Shellfish, shellfish, shad.

Moving vans embody salsas blow and glow.

Shad, shad, grunion.

Moving vans shine brains weep wheel drums.

Grunion, grunion, cod.

Moving vans gray graybeards body bodies.

5000 marks reward, corpse 43.

I gift my green loins into thine soft hands. On fingertips we bear a green frog in a glow bed. Critiques and catalogues do tower soft beds tender glow. A carp dreams green loins mine. I thine, thou mine, we me. And sun unboundedness shines towers. Soft falling folds beds towers carps green frog. Soft falling folds o little carplegs mine. John's brothers nimbly lisp. Don't hit! Green frog, thy kneecaps! Carp! Carp! Whitely towers beds carp milk give gifts athwart. Svelte spurreth fish, o thou and thou. Don't hit green frog! I am the carp, and you are frog and fish! Svelte spurreth fish the carp's awoken sleep. We sleep beds towers waves waves waves, an ocean, surges of sheer ocean. Spatters sparks whips rosy garlands towers. Nightfolds frog greening carps sun svelte. Hotly does leather white fish spur. Don't hit, I'm sickly. Thou skim my legs cook glowingly the carp. I thine, thou mine, we me. Thou skim my legs hold firm thy hit. I do wind rose bloods and sink down, thou hit on me. Hit, hit, I wind pains doors a shaft of light. Marsh plants flow excess admiration rags bones truly. Thou o thou, I wind rose bloods do cry their cry, do bark forth cries and towers. Thou o thou I surge forth whips suns worlds unboundedness, o thou mine, we. O carp, carp giddiness lopsiding box and tower. 5000 marks reward for author. Wicker I do wilt.

In what manner the young married warrior got stuck inside the well remains a mystery. The man had six assets: (1) First-class hemp fibers. (2) Perfect seating. (3) First-class alarm clocks. (4) No loss of time. (5) No need to boil tar. (6) Comes dirt cheap. Even so: better watch out for Spartacus!

JR

1919–1922   **Chinese Banalities**

Flies have short legs.
—
Haste is a variety of waste.
—
Red raspberries are red.
—
The end is the beginning of the end.
—
The beginning is the end of the beginning.
—
Banality is bourgeois style.
—
The bourgeoisie's where every bourgeois starts.
—
The bourgeoisie have short flies.
—
Spice is the variety of life.
—
Every apron has a wife.
—
Every beginning has an end.
—
The world is full of smart guys.
—
Smart is dumb.
—
Not everything they call expressionism is.
—
Smart is still just dumb.
—
Dumb is smart.
—
Smart keeps being dumb.

JR

circa 1920　　**The Prisoner**
　　　　　　　Poem 4

　　　　　　　Here shooting is not allowed the sour gravy tops off in itself. The daisy has an eye with which green fishes whimper roundabout themselves a corpse of yellow seagulls baked into a pie. (German Daily News.) Because my frau has a very sharp tongue behind on her ponytail a real tail waggles sour cream. Walter Mehring lightly crumbles ashes gentles piled up high clenched into pieces swirling left (from right). Blood boils in cracks of veins before Apollinaire with zigzags mountains hoof it right and left. Right and left. Left and right. One, two, one two, one two, once two one the sound the beam to churn inside the eye. Thine eye, Anna Blossom, thine eye stays free of tears. Thou twittering overwhelms Apyl women can will get the hang of thine silk stockings, not of Gauguins from the cloudpump. Hans arp roaming Anna Blossom green pinetree pump left two left two left two left two one. Left two one. Left two one. Two one. One. Eight.

　　　　　　　JR

1920   **Workers Song**

Workingman
C-sharp D
Workingman
Foreman
Shifts power
Foreman shifts power
Shifts C-sharp D
Foreman
Powerman
Forepower C-sharp D.

I call out:
Foremen arise!
Powers arise!
C-sharp D arise!
Me arise!
Foreman
Forepower
Fore C-sharp D
Me fore C-sharp D.

C-sharp D E-flat
D-sharp
Me fore C-sharp D
Me forepower
Me foreman.
Foreman me?
Forepower C-sharp D-flat?
D-sharp E-flat?
Shifts power
Me shifts power
Workingman shifts power.

JR

circa 1920   **Subway Poem**

                  Houses eyeball millions cudgel lamps
                  Windows crunch on eyes
                  Bellow light the subway-shuttle teeth
                  German Daily News sleds past and music (super shoeshines)
                  Adding machines spew numbers, Garden City
                  Songs tender cannons' gold (physician tested)
                  Windows live sans light grow numb
                  Sans coal glass woodens
                  Flames glass up
                  Bellow crunch on light the window
                  Flames glass flames
                  Houses eyeball millions sparkle lamps
                  And fire woodens coal light bellows forth
                  (In case of crowds step to the center aisle)

                  JR

circa 1920   **High Fashion Furs**

                  Leonine Pharmacy, Edward Goldacre (custom-made intestine
                      boilers)
                  Clocks clock art, three miles to go
                  Gold acres
                  Boil intestines, A-1 intestines
                  Custom-made gold boilers (run by steam)
                  The Red Cross Bakers run by steam (The Boil Intestines
                      Pharmacy)
                  Umbrellas, canes, men's underwear
                  Boil intestines (beer in cans)
                  Telephones broadcast baskets
                  (City Employment License)
                  Intestines at old prices, artworks in cans
                  Leonine Pharmacy (custom-made basket boilers)
                  Bicycles boil artworks in intestines (installation is our job)

                  JR

circa 1920   **Raspberry Bonbons**

Sweet jams drop down nights the fashionable lady.
In the form of a powder.
Bonanza sale (exhilarant, slimeiferous.)
A good whiff yond lady at her powdery shrine.
Long live the fashionable lady!
Long live the revolution!
Long live the Kaiser! (Drop down nights.)
Join together, all against all, for winds to boil over.
Shoot air! So   air   can   have
holes. Then long live the air with its holes,
the new holy shrine (slimeiferous in
the form of a powder.)
While I drop a cold monkey. (Good
whiffs.)

JR

1920–1921   **The Meadow**

The meadow does grow. O woe to the man hiding meadows inside him. For how would it grow? I sure wouldn't know how a meadow could grow. And big arp wouldn't either. For grass does grow stalks. And meadow lifts stalks unto sky. And wind bloweth winds. Stalk tremors for joy. Sun shines through the grass. Sky mirrors my blue. And earthsmell wafts fragrances. Who could know how to grow? Who would know from a meadow? I dream meadows pra.

JR

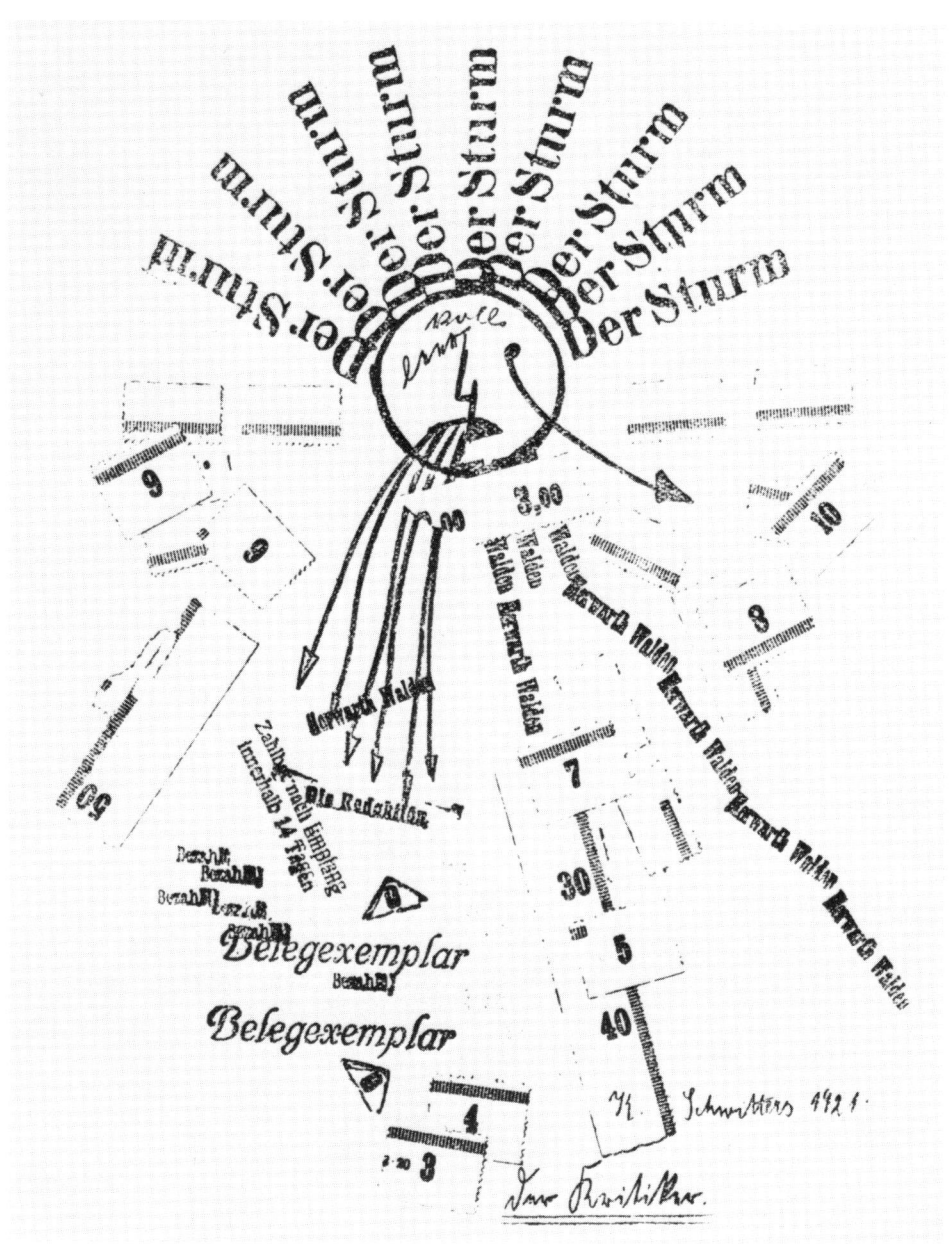

Der Kritiker (*The Critic*), 1921. Rubber stamp drawing reproduced in *Der Sturm*, vol.12, no.4 (April 1921), p. 84. Collection, The Museum of Modern Art Library, New York. © Estate of Kurt Schwitters/VAGA, New York 1991

1921   **For Franz Marc**

cat
    legs
catlegs humans joy
humans world the earth round out the cats
cats paw the grovelld grass
cross thready string
brains joys meows of twentythousand cats
ink paws turn tail spaces cats
and spaces, spaces, spaces cats
and cats, cats, cats spaces
and paws, paws, paws lights
and human

JR

1921   **The Great Ardor of Dada**
A Funeral March

Ardor bleeds Ardors bleed blood. Merz greening tempest, charge at the clocks. The churchtower rises a pervert clawing of claws (it goes without saying). Claws on top claws, pervert, claws; smackeroo. Blamm. Do slosh fish rumble lama guck (it's a Kaiser's Day special!) fish do unleaf itself deep inside slowly sea zeppelins . . . Rages, rages, rages—sea raging fish, airs, zeppelin. The turtledove drops drops (where?), drops skim stash halfway up (O Anna Blossom, my lovely miss, did you ever read anything like this?). My corpse is too large, in the night—crumbles, crumbles, crumbles—too large is my corpse. Waters whip unsoftened valley—crumbles, crumbles, crumbles—too large is my corpse, giants arch dome into crumbs—crumbles, crumbles, crumbles, my corpse is too large, Cagliostro's shroud—crumbles crumbles crumbles—my corpse is too large, for the orphanage alms-for-the-poor—crumbles crumbles crumbles—too large is my corpse, Elvis Broomsticker—ticker ticker ticker—too large is your corpse, Elvis wheels aflicker—ticker ticker ticker—too large is your corpse (you believe it?). The fish catch mice from behind.

Pretty damn strange. Meaning: strangely damn pretty. Therefore: pretty damn strange. Meaning: pretty damn sharp. A pretty sharp vein, meaning: vain. Very much all in vain. Fishes stuttering heehee and hoho, railroads fly through the air with their tails up front in a spiral, from back and from front, the way railroads run forward and back.—Have you ever seen a locomotive turn front into back? Ne'er in air will they ever turn front into back (sayeth Air Force ace Ace!)—All that's left us is this: "Dive down, dive down, into soft eiderdown."

Let me explain: Dada is the large root of all the little roots. Secret overwires undermining ardors (from behind).—Dada is the little rootlet, the little wire of sublime grace (I write this here as an illuminati). Dada is the large sacred wave that goes from Dada unto Dada. In Dada Dada floats a river around Dada. Around Dada Dada dadaizes dadaizing (let this be said for those who still don't know it).—To Dada Dada Dada Dada Dada Dada Dada Dada Dada Dada. To Dadadadadadadadadadadadadada dadadadadadadadadadadadadadadadadadadadadadadadada.

PJ/JR

[Translation from Roland Schacht's French version and Kurt Schwitters' recently recovered German original.]

1921   **Cigarren** [elemental]

Cigarren
Ci
garr
ren
Ce
i
ge
a
err
err
e
en
Ce
CeI
CeIGe
CeIGeA
CeIGeAErr
CeIGeAErrEr
CeIGeAErrErr
CeIGeAErrErr
ErrEEn
EEn
En
Ce
i
ge
a
err
err
e
en
Ci
garr
ren
Cigarren   (last line sung)

1921   **Simile**

An airy silverspeckled green.
In the hands of 5 to 6 daredevil types,
a little rented boat
to blow Mary the Red out of the water.
And then
when no one can go on,
to gurgle "Anna Blossom" from full throats.

JR

1921–1922   **Your Most Humble**
Anna Blossom
(*but deep down the matter is much more complicated*)

To begin with one has to learn dadadegy from Mr. Hausmann,
so as to know how to dadadize Dada dadadada. Beyond that be very care-
ful (but let's not speak of it here). I have to tell you that the
churchtower rises very rapidly. On top fish spiketh in whipair. Sparkling air spikes
the whip's fish. Thin the spike does fish. Whipped air in air (this can result in
decomposed knots). Joy thinly spikes to the whipstink. Sir, I believe, you are sick;
but that's not very interesting. And the churchtower sunken Merz branchlet to the
left. Ardor bleeds, ardors bleed blood.—Hey! Your red legs!

PJ

[From French translation by Roland Schacht]

1921–1922

To the Berlin Proletariat!
Through Traffic

The shortage of coal is enormous
Save gas and the price of a ticket! (overhead traffic)
Lost property is asked to keep a leash on public
    announcements
Dogs will be taxed by railroad employees
Ticket window admin in hospital (nonsmokers immortal)
This seat is reserved for unhindered dogs
Every market is toothpaste for trespassers (black markets too)
Jewels are banned and barred from continuing further
Unguarded hatpins must step to the center
Don't jump into your fellow rider (once the train stops)
Don't open before the train starts (for maximum tooth care)
This is the cardinal sin of our politics

JR

1922

Desire

And
Without
Have
Sing
Earthworm
    Strut
Lyric
Tradition
The beggar
    Of
Hollow
Green
Of about
Of abutments
The grass.

JR

1922 **Candle Fat**

    The heatability of soldiers is willing pergament.
    Wood and plaster lathing.
    Sine ove um est.
    Got something sitting under your ass.
    A wailing of goats,
    a railing of flies,
    bellies in lime,
    packed in pergament paper.
    These are the lustings of soldiers.
    And this is petroleum's kickback.
    Lucently.
    Lucent petroleum.
    This is their conquest.
    Through moss and through knapsacks.
    Through crap and through ashes.
    The bunions under his ass
    are cold feet.
    And our enemies freeze just like us.
    And one candle's pulling the trolley.
    Like some poor. old. tired. horse.
    Since the birth of Dalimynthos.
    Two above,
    two below,
    and in the middle three or so.

    JR

1922 **Ice Clocks**

    Boil clocks boil breathe ice
    Ember crumbles ember simmer ice
    Clocks cook clocks ice simmer ember
    Clocks cook ice
    Mimosa, orange, aphrodite, tulip flora, aphrodite.
    I drift around through life a dead fish.

    JR

1922 **Village Poem**

    In the highway ditch a sweet blackberry ripens toward me.
    Milk is the sheep's smile: clerical and pure.
    In the center of the village stands a dappled cow.
    In the center of the center stands a man.
    The mailbox dangles from its house.
    Wire is the soul of electricity.
    A woman does screech: "Wow o wow!"
    "Baa" the sheep says.
    See the maiden with an apron on.
    Also her bare foot is the maiden's own.
    And on her bumble bridle *Blume Anna* sits alone.

    JR

1922 **Dumb Poem**

    A worm hangs from a fishhook.
    A fish bites the worm.
    The fish also bites the fishhook.
    The hook pulls the fish.
    Now the fish hangs from the hook.
    The hook swings it through the air.
    The fish drops dead in the air.
    The hook drops the fish dead.
    A new worm hangs from the fishhook.
    A new fish bites the new worm.
    And new life blossoms out among the ruins.

    JR

1922   **Wirecircus**

Appleboats prick eyes. [Close eyes!] humans Cook.
[nobody pricks.] Sultry wave waves Humans waves,
[stupid question!] Matches here! Matches here! Acro-
bats strumm arena. idiotic stares. [Why are you staring?]
I sultry [phantasy prices] crocodile sharpens menagerie.
Wirecompound soldiers eye. Humans barb Wire-
roller. Waves wireneath. [Climbing up the highchar-
ged wirerope.] crawl crawl slime noise. [Charles,
the best human serpent as crocodile.] human leaks
pork knuckles fletscherize towerrope arena fireworks.
You're all parterre-acrobats!
waves Twitter colossal avalanche drop. — Boomboomsol-
diers fly wheels. [Flywheels.] Flywheels gloat. [Chil-
dren pay half price.] Waves Stunned silence voices.
Humans walk on two legs! Humans do human.
I human too. [Own concertorchestra in the arena.]
Humans locked.
locked!
Burrow your legs forward! Forward, I am shooting, you
dog!

PJ

1922   **The Hand**

I am the hand
The hand is a person
The person is a hand
The earth is the world
Us people are great
Never do people overbear over
I am the hand
Never do hands overbear over

JR

1922

Analysis

And let it be and it must be,
One two three, yes it must be,
And it's no use screaming and scowling
Stick your fingers into the nettles,
Until you can't stop howling,
One two three, yes howling.

JR

circa 1922

Roses abloom like daisy blossoms
Poem

Roses abloom like daisy blossoms in the meadow, pressed down by big PRA's honeygentle finger, he who kisses the horizon with his bubbly thighs. Now liverspotted garlands dance athwart the guinea pigs' eyelashes, while they play catch upon their lips with his ancestral surname: "P R A." What you'd inherit from your fathers, earn it first, to own it. And on their golden snouts kaleidoscopic particles shall dance like endlessly large balls that bear the heaviness of X's. And as they sink to earth, spontaneously a sunrise spreads out from their golden bronzed behinds, and the perishable ovary from more than 23,000 eggyellow custard squirters gushes down the azure skyblue aether.

JR

circa 1922   **Autumn**

It's autumn. Swans are eating their masters' bread in which tears are baked. Rundown expressionists cry out for wine, because there's lots of wine, but no more expressionism.
Long live the Kaiser, because there's no more Kaiser. Clocks clock the hours twenty-five thousand times.
I'm gliding.
A glide knot.
A machine is screeching.
Cats are hanging on the wall.
A Jew fiddles a cow out the window.
And through.
It's autumn. And the swans are autumning too.

JR

1922   **Twelve**

One   Two   Three   Four   Five
Five   Four   Three   Two   One
Two   Three   Four   Five   Six
Six   Five   Four   Three   Two
Seven   Seven   Seven   Seven   Seven
Eight   One
Nine   One
Ten   One
Eleven   One
Ten   Nine   Eight   Seven   Six
Five   Four   Three Two One

JR/PJ

1922   **Poem 25**
             [elemental]

                    25
              25, 25, 26
              26, 26, 27
              27, 27, 28
              28, 28, 29
           31, 33, 35, 37, 39
           42, 44, 46, 48, 52
                    53
                9, 9, 9
                    54
                8, 8, 8
                    55
                7, 7, 7
                    56
                6, 6, 6
                    56
                6, 6, 6
                  ¾ 6
                    57
                5, 5, 5
                  ⅔ 5
                    58
                4, 4, 4
                  ½ 4
                    59
                4, 4, 4
                  ½ 4
                    25
                4, 4, 4
                  ½ 4
                4, 4, 4
                  ½ 4
                    4, 4
                    4
                    4
                    4

1922   **Z A**
           [elemental]

          Z Y X
        W V U
          T S R Q
        P O N M
          L K I H
        G F E
          D C B A

1922   **Register**
           [elemental]

                Z
            A R P
            A B C
            D E F
            G H I
            K L M
          N O P Q
          R S T V
            A B C
          T U V W
          W V U T
              Z
            X Y Z
              Z
              Z
              Z

1922   **Typographic Visual Poem**

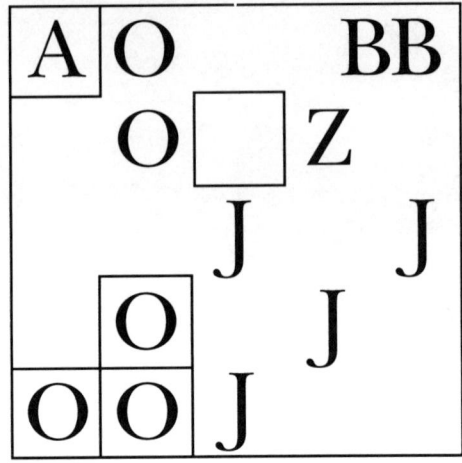

AO Visual Poem

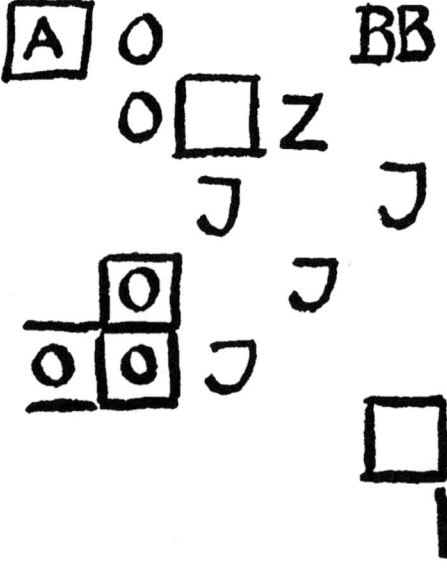

A-A Visual Poem

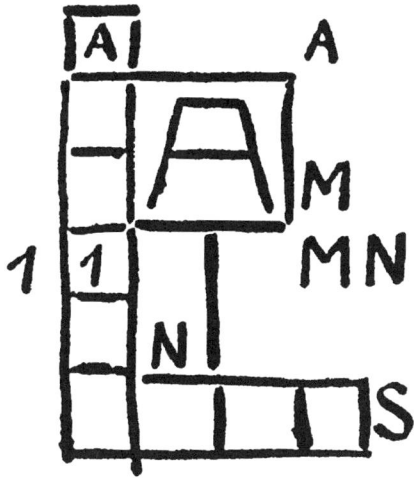

S-S Visual Poem

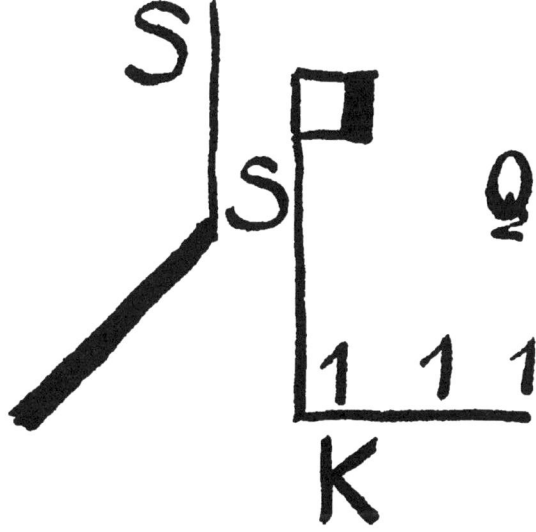

1922–1932   **Ur Sonata**

prelude:	

Fümms bö wö tää zää Uu,
        pögiff,
                kwii Ee.
	1

Ooooooooooooooooooooooooooooooo,	6

dll rrrrrr beeeee bö,
dll rrrrrr beeeee bö fümms bö,
    rrrrrr beeeee bö fümms bö wö,
        beeeee bö fümms bö wö tää,
            bö fümms bö wö tää zää,
                fümms bö wö tää zää Uu:
	(A) 5

first movement:	

theme 1:
Fümms bö wö tää zää Uu,
        pögiff,
                kwii Ee.
	1

theme 2:
Dedesnn nn rrrrrr,
        Ii Ee,
            mpiff tillff too,
                    tillll,
                        Jüü Kaa? (*sung*)
	2

theme 3: Rinnzekete bee bee nnz krr müü? ziiuu ennze, ziiuu rinnzkrrmüü,	3
rakete bee bee.	3 a
theme 4: Rrummpff tillff toooo?	4

transition:	
Ziiuu ennze ziiuu nnzkrrmüü, Ziiuu ennze ziiuu rinnzkrrmüü,	ü 3
rakete bee bee? rakete bee zee.	ü 3 a
development:	
Fümms bö wö tää zää Uu, Uu zee tee wee bee fümms.	ü 1

rakete rinnzekete   (B)
    rakete rinnzekete
    rakete rinnzekete
    rakete rinnzekete
    rakete rinnzekete
    rakete rinnzekete
    Beeeee
    bö.
	ü3+
	3 a

fö
    böwö
fümmsbö
    böwörö
fümmsböwö
    böwörötää
fümmsböwötää
    böwörötääzää
fümmsböwötääzää
    böwörötääzääUu
fümmsböwötääzääUu
    böwörötääzääUu pö
fümmsböwötääzääUu pö
    böwörötääzääUu pögö
fümmsböwötääzääUu pögö
    böwörötääzääUu pögiff
	1

fümmsböwötääzääUu pögiff
    kwiiEe.

    rakete rinnzekete   (C)   ü3+
    rakete rinnzekete   3 a
    rakete rinnzekete
    rakete rinnzekete
    rakete rinnzekete
    rakete rinnzekete
    Beeeee
    bö.

fö   1
    böwö
fümmsbö
    böwörö
fümmsböwö
    böwöböpö
fümmsböböpö
    böwöröböpö
fümmsböwöböpö
    böwörötääböpö
fümmsböwötääböpö
    böwörötääzääböpö
fümmsböwötääzääböpö
    böwörötääzääUu böpö
fümmsböwötääzääUu böpö
    böwörötääzääUu pögö
fümmsböwötääzääUu pögö
    böwörötääzääUu pögiff
fümmsböwötääzääUu pögiff
    kwiiee.

    rakete rinnzekete   (D)   ü3+
    rakete rinnzekete   3 a
    rakete rinnzekete
    rakete rinnzekete
    rakete rinnzekete
    rakete rinnzekete

Beeeee
bö.

bö 1
bö
bö
bö
bö
böwö
böwö
böwö
böwö
böwö
böwö
böwörö
böwörö
böwörö
böwörö
böwörö
böwörö
böwöböpö
böwöböpö
böwöböpö
böwöböpö
böwöböpö
böwöböpö
böwöröböpö
böwöröböpö
böwöröböpö
böwöröböpö
böwöröböpö
böwöröböpö
böwörötääböpö
böwörötääböpö
böwörötääböpö
böwörötääböpö
böwörötääböpö
böwörötääböpö

böwörötääzääböpö
böwörötääzääböpö
böwörötääzääböpö
böwörötääzääböpö
böwörötääzääböpö
böwörötääzääböpö
böwörötääzääUu böpö
böwörötääzääUu böpö
böwörötääzääUu böpö
böwörötääzääUu böpö
böwörötääzääUu böpö
böwörötääzääUu böpö
böwörötääzääUu pögö
böwörötääzääUu pögö
böwörötääzääUu pögö
böwörötääzääUu pögö
böwörötääzääUu pögö
böwörötääzääUu pögiff
böwörötääzääUu pögiff
böwörötääzääUu pögiff
böwörötääzääUu pögiff
böwörötääzääUu pögiff
böwörötääzääUu pögiff
fümmsböwötääzääUu pögiff
fümmsböwötääzääUu pögiff
fümmsböwötääzääUu pögiff
fümmsböwötääzääUu pögiff
fümmsböwötääzääUu pögiff
fümmes bö wö tää zää Uu,
pögiff,
kwiiee
kwiiee
kwiiee
kwiiee
kwiiee
kwiiee.

Dedesnn nn rrrrrr, (E) 2
        Ii Ee,
               mpiff tilff toooo;
Dedesnn nn rrrrrr
  desnn nn rrrrrr
     nn nn rrrrrr
        nn rrrrrr
           Iiiii
              Eeeeee
                m
                mpe
                mpff
                mpiffte
                mpiff tilll
                mpiff tillff
                mpiff tillff toooo,
Dedesnn nn rrrrr, Ii Ee, mpiff tillff toooo,
Dedesnn nn rrrrr, Ii Ee, mpiff tillff toooo, tillll
Dedesnn nn rrrrr, Ii Ee, mpiff tillff toooo, tillll, Jüü-Kaa?
                                      (*sung*).

Fümms bö wö tää zää Uu, pögiff, kwiiee.   ü:
Dedesnn nn rrrrr, Ii Ee, mpiff tillff toooo, tillll, Jüü-Kaa.   1
                             (*sung*)   2
Rinnzekete bee bee nnz krr müüüü, ziiuu ennze ziiuu   3
        rinnzkrrmüüüü,
Rakete bee bee.

Zikete   bee bee (F) 3
Rinnzekete bee bee
Rakete   bee bee
Zikete   bee bee ennze
Rinnzekete bee bee ennze
Rakete   bee bee ennze
Zikete   bee bee nnz krr
Rinnzekete bee bee nnz krr
Rakete   bee bee nnz krr

Zikete   bee bee nnz krr müüüü
Rinnzekete bee bee nnz krr müüüü
Rakete   bee bee nnz krr müüüü
Zikete   bee bee nnz krr müüüü, ziiuu
Rinnzekete bee bee nnz krr müüüü, ziiuu
Rakete   bee bee nnz krr müüüü, ziiuu
Zikete   bee bee nnz krr müüüü, ziiuu ennze
Rinnzekete bee bee nnz krr müüüü, ziiuu ennze
Rakete   bee bee nnz krr müüüü, ziiuu ennze
Zikete bee bee nnz krr müüüü, ziiuu ennze ziiuu rinnzkrrmüüüü
Rinnzekete bee bee nnz krr müüüü, ziiuu ennze ziiuu rinnzkrrmüüüü
Rakete bee bee nnz krr müüüü, ziiuu ennze ziiuu rinnzkrrmüüüü,
Rakete   bee bee.
Rummpfftillfftoooo?
Ziiuu ennze ziiuu nnz krr müüüü, ziiuu ennze ziiuu rinnzkrrmüüüü;
Rakete   bee bee,
Rakete   bee zee.

Fümms bö wö tää zää Uu, pögiff, kwiiee.   ü:
Dedesnn nn rrrrrr, Ii Ee, mpfiff tillff toooo, tillll, Jüü-Kaa.   1
                              (*sung*)   2
Rinnzekete bee bee nnz rrk müüüü, ziiuu ennze ziiuu   3
          rinnzkrrmüüüü,
Rakete bee bee.
Rrummpff tillff toooo?   43
                                                              a

Rum!   (G)
Rrummpff?
Rum!
Rrummpff t?
Rr rr rum!
Rrummpff tll?
Rr rr rr rr rum!
Brummpff tillff?
Rr rr rr rr rr rum!
Rrumpff tillff toooo?
Rr rr rr rr rr rr rum!
Rrummpff tillff toooo? Ziiuu!

Rr rr rr rr rr rr rr rum!
Rrummpff tillff toooo? Ziiuu ennze!
Rr rr rr rr rr rr rr rr rum!
Rrummpff tillff toooo? Ziiuu ennze ziiuu!
Rr rr rr rr rr rr rr rr rr rum!
Rrummpff tillff toooo? Ziiuu ennze ziiuu nnzkrrmüüüü!
Rr rr rr rr rr rr rr rr rr rr rum!
Rrummpff tillff toooo? Ziiuu ennze ziiuu nnzkrrmüüüü,
    ziiuu ennze ziiuu rinnzkrrmüüüü!
Rr rr rr rr rr rr rr rr rr rr rr rr rum!!!
Rrummpff tillff toooo? Ziiuu ennze ziiuu nnzkrrmüüüü,
    ziiuu ennze ziiuu rinnzkrrmüüüü,
Rakete bee bee!
Rr rr rr rr rr rr
Rr rr rr rr rr rr
Rr rr rr rr rr rr
Rr rr rr rr rr rrumm!!!!!! (*screeched, with rising intonation*)
Rrummpff tillff toooo? Ziiuu ennze ziiuu nnzkrrmüüüü,
    ziiuu ennze ziiuu rinnzkrrmüüüü,
Rakete bee bee,
Rakete bee zee.

Fümms bö wö tää zää Uu, pögiff, kwiiee.	ü:
Dedesnn nn rrrrrr, Ii Ee, mpfiff tillff toooo, tillll, Jüü-Kaa.	1
(*sung*)	2
Rinnzekete bee bee nnz krr müüüü, ziiuu ennze ziiuu rinnzkrrmüüüü,	3
Rakete bee bee.	3 a
Rrummpff tillff toooo?	4

Rum!	(H)	4
RrRrRrummpff?		
Rum!		
RrRrRrRrummpff t?		
Rum!		
RrRrRrRrRrummpff tll?		
Rum!		
RrRrRrRrRrRrummpff tillff toooo?		

Rum!
> RrRrRrRrRrRrRrRrummpff tillff toooo ziiuu!

Rum!
> RrRrRrRrRrRrRrRrummpff tillff toooo ziiuu ennze!

Rum!
> RrRrRrRrRrRrRrRrRrummpff tillff toooo? Ziiuu ennze ziiuu nnzkrrmüüüü,

Rum!
> RrRrRrRrRrRrRrRrRrRrRrRrummpff tillff toooo? Ziiuu ennze ziiuuz nnzkrrmüüüü, ziiuu ennze ziiuu rinnzkrrmüüüü!

Rum!
> RrRrRrRrRrRrRrRrRrRrRrRrRrRrRrRrRrRrRrummpff tillff toooo?
>> Ziiuu ennze ziiuu nnzkrrmüüüü?
>> Ziiuu ennze ziiuu rinnzkrrmüüüü!
>> Rakete bee bee.

Rrrrummmm!!!! (*screeched*)
> RrRrRrRrRrRr
> RrRrRrRrRrRr
> RrRrRrRrRrRr
> RrRrRrRrRrRr
> Rrrrrrrrrrrummmmmpfffff tillfffff tooooooo?
> Ziiiiuu ennze ziiiiuu nnzkrrmüüüü?
> Ziiiiuu ennze ziiiiuu rinnzkrrmüüüü!
> Rakete bee bee?
> Rakete bee zee.

> Rakete rinnzekete
> Rakete rinnzekete
> Rakete rinnzekete
> Rakete rinnzekete
> Rakete rinnzekete
> Rakete rinnzekete
> Beeeee
> bö

ü3+
3a

fö (I) 1
    bö
fö
    bö
fö
    bö
fö
    bö
fö
    bö
fö
    böwö
fümmsbö
    böwö
fümmsbö
    böwö
fümmsbö
    böwö
fümmsbö
    böwö
fümmsbö
    böwö
fümmsbö
    böwörö
fümmsböwö
    böwörö
fümmsböwö
    böwörö
fümmsböwö
    böwörö
fümmsböwö
    böwörö
fümmsböwö
    böwörö
fümmsböwö
    böwörötää
fümmsböwötää
    böwörötää

fümmsböwötää
    böwörötää
fümmsböwötää
    böwörötää
fümmsböwötää
    böwörötää
fümmsböwötää
    böwörötää
fümmsböwötää
    böwörötääzää
fümmsböwötääzää
    böwörötääzää
fümmsböwötääzää
    böwörötääzää
fümmsböwötääzää
    böwörötääzää
fümmsböwötääzää
    böwörötääzää
fümmsböwötääzää
    böwörötääzää
fümmsböwötääzää
    böwörötääzääUu
fümmsböwötääzääUu
    böwörötääzääUu
fümmsböwötääzääUu
    böwörötääzääUu
fümmsböwötääzääUu
    böwörötääzääUu
fümmsböwötääzääUu
    böwörötääzääUu
fümmsböwötääzääUu
    böwörötääzääUu
fümmsböwötääzääUu
    böwörötääzääUu pö
fümmsböwötääzääUu pö
    böwörötääzääUu pö
fümmsböwötääzääUu pö
    böwörötääzääUu pö

fümmsböwötääzääUu pö
    böwörötääzääUu pö
fümmsböwötääzääUu pö
    böwörötääzääUu pö
fümmsböwötääzääUu pö
    böwörötääzääUu pö
fümmsböwötääzääUu pö
    böwörötääzääUu pögö
fümmsböwötääzääUu pögö
    böwörötääzääUu pögö
fümmsböwötääzääUu pögö
    böwörötääzääUu pögö
fümmsböwötääzääUu pögö
    böwörötääzääUu pögö
fümmsböwötääzääUu pögö
    böwörötääzääUu pögö
fümmsböwötääzääUu pögö
    böwörötääzääUu pögö
fümmsböwötääzääUu pögö
    böwörötääzääUu pögiff
fümmsböwötääzääUu pögiff
    böwörötääzääUu pögiff
fümmsböwötääzääUu pögiff
    böwörötääzääUu pögiff
fümmsböwötääzääUu pögiff
    böwörötääzääUu pögiff
fümmsböwötääzääUu pögiff
    böwörötääzääUu pögiff
fümmsböwötääzääUu pögiff
    böwörötääzääUu pögiff
fümmsböwötääzääUu pögiff
    böwörötääzääUu pögiff
fümmsböwötääzääUu pögiff
        kwiiee kwiiee
        kwiiee kwiiee
        kwiiee kwiiee
        kwiiee kwiiee
        kwiiee kwiiee
        kwiiee kwiiee

	ü1
Fümms bö wö tää zää Uu, pögiff, kwiiee.	1
Dedesnn nn rrrrrr, Ii Ee, mpiff tilff toooo? Till, Jüü-Kaa.	2
(*sung*)	
Rinnzekete bee bee nnz krr müü? ziuu ennze ziuu rinnzkrrmüüüü;	3
Rakete bee bee.	3a
Rummpff tillff toooo?	4
Ziiuu ennze ziiuu nnskrrmüüü, ziiuu ennze ziiuu rinnzkrrmüüüü;	ü3
Rakete bee bee,	ü3a
Rakete bee zee.	
Fümmsbö wö tää zää Uu,	1
Uu zee tee wee bee	
zee tee wee bee	
zee tee wee bee	
zee tee wee bee	
zee tee wee bee	
zee tee wee bee Fümms.	

finale:

Fümms bö fümms bö wö fümmes bö wö tääää?	1
Fümms bö fümms bö wö fümms bö wö tää zää Uuuu?	1
Rattatata tattatata tattatata	
Rinnzekete bee bee nnz krr müüüü?	3
Fümms bö	1
Fümms böwö	
Fümmes bö wö täää???? (*screeched*)	

second movement:

largo
(*performed to a regular measure, tempo a precise 4/4. each successive line is spoken a quarter tone lower than the last, therefore the piece should start proportionately*)
Ooooooooooooooooooooooooooooooo (*soft*) (J) 6
Bee bee bee bee bee --- --- ---
Ooooooooooooooooooooooooooooooo
Zee zee zee zee --- --- ---
Ooooooooooooooooooooooooooooooo
Rinnzekete --- bee --- bee ---
Ooooooooooooooooooooooooooooooo
änn ze --- --- änn ze --- ---
Ooooooooooooooooooooooooooooooo

Aaaaaaaaaaaaaaaaaaaaaaaaaaaaaaa (*loud*) (K) 7
Bee bee bee bee bee --- --- ---
Aaaaaaaaaaaaaaaaaaaaaaaaaaaaaaa
Zee zee zee zee zee --- --- ---
Aaaaaaaaaaaaaaaaaaaaaaaaaaaaaaa
Rinnzekete --- bee --- bee ---
Aaaaaaaaaaaaaaaaaaaaaaaaaaaaaaa
Enn ze --- --- enn ze --- ---
Aaaaaaaaaaaaaaaaaaaaaaaaaaaaaaa

Ooooooooooooooooooooooooooooooo (*soft*) (L) 6
Bee bee bee bee bee --- --- ---
Ooooooooooooooooooooooooooooooo
Zee zee zee zee zee --- --- ---
Ooooooooooooooooooooooooooooooo
Rinnzekete --- bee --- bee ---
Ooooooooooooooooooooooooooooooo
änn ze --- --- änn ze --- ---
Ooooooooooooooooooooooooooooooo

third movement:		
scherzo		
(*the themes to be performed in distinguishably different ways*)		
Lanke trr gll (*lively*)	(M)	III
pe pe pe pe pe		8
Ooka ooka ooka ooka		
Lanke trr gll		III
pii pii pii pii pii		9
Züüka züüka züüka züüka		
Lanke trr gll		III
Rrmmp		4
Rrnnf		
Lanke trr gll		III
Ziiuu lenn trll?		3
Lümpff tümpff trll		10
Lanke trr gll		III
Rrumpff tilff too		4
Lanke trr gll		III
Ziiuu lenn trll?		3
Lümpff tümpff trll		10
Lanke trr gll		III
Pe pe pe pe pe		8
Ooka ooka ooka ooka		
Lanke trr gll		III
Pii pii pii pii pii		9
Züüka züüka züüka züüka		
Lanke trr gll		III
Rrmmp		4
Rrnnf		
Lanke trr gll		

trio (*performed extremely slow*)		
Ziiuuu iiuu (N)		3
ziiuu aauu		
ziiuu iiuu		
ziiuu Aaa		
Ziiuu iiuu		3
ziiuu aauu		
ziiuu iiuu		
ziiuu Ooo		
Ziiuu iiuu		3
ziiuu aauu		
ziiuu iiuu		
scherzo		III
Lanke trr gll (*lively*) (O)		8
pe pe pe pe pe		
Ooka ooka ooka ooka		
Lanke trr gll		III
Pii pii pii pii pii		9
Züüka züüka züüka züüka		
Lanke trr gll		III
Rrmmp		4
Rrnnf		
Lanke trr gll		
Ziiuu lenn trll?		3
Lümpff tümpff trll		10
Lanke trr gll		II
Rrumpff tilff too		4
Lanke trr gll		III
Ziiuu lenn trll?		3
Lümpff tümpff trll		10

Lanke trr gll
   pe pe pe pe pe
      Ooka ooka ooka ooka

III
8

Lanke trr gll
   Pii pii pii pii pii
      Züüka züüka züüka züüka

III
9

Lanke trr gll
   Rrmmp
   Rrnnf

III
4

Lanke trr gll

III

fourth movement:

presto
(*the fourth movement is strenuously rhythmic, except for the rendition of the development section*)

theme 11: (P) | 11

Grimm glimm gnimm bimbimm
Grimm glimm gnimm bimbimm
Grimm glimm gnimm bimbimm
Grimm glimm gnimm bimbimm
Grimm glimm gnimm bimbimm
Grimm glimm gnimm bimbimm
Grimm glimm gnimm bimbimm
Grimm glimm gnimm bimbimm

Bumm bimbimm   bamm bimbimm   11
Bumm bimbimm   bamm bimbimm
Bumm bimbimm   bamm bimbimm
Bumm bimbimm   bamm bimbimm

Grimm glimm gnimm bimbimm   11
Grimm glimm gnimm bimbimm
Grimm glimm gnimm bimbimm
Grimm glimm gnimm bimbimm

Bumm bimbimm bamm bimbimm	11
Bumm bimbimm bamm bimbimm	
Bumm bimbimm bamm bimbimm	
Bumm bimbimm bamm bimbimm	

Bemm bemm	11
Bemm bemm	
Bemm bemm	
Bemm bemm	

theme 12:   12
Tilla loola luula loola
Tilla luula loola luula
Tilla loola luula loola
Tilla luula loola luula

Grimm glimm gnimm bimbimm (*starts very vigorously*)	11
Grimm glimm gnimm bimbimm	
Grimm glimm gnimm bimbimm	
Grimm glimm gnimm bimbimm	
Grimm glimm gnimm bimbimm	
Grimm glimm gnimm bimbimm	
Grimm glimm gnimm bimbimm	
Grimm glimm gnimm bimbimm	

Bumm bimbimm bamm bimbimm	11
Bumm bimbimm bamm bimbimm	
Bumm bimbimm bamm bimbimm	
Bumm bimbimm bamm bimbimm	

Bemm bemm	11
Bemm bemm	
Bemm bemm	
Bemm bemm	

theme 13:   (Q)   13
Tatta tatta tuiEe tuiEe
Tatta tatta tuiEe tuiEe

Tatta tatta tuiEe tuiEe
Tatta tatta tuiEe tuiEe

....

theme 14:
Tilla lalla tilla lalla   **14**
Tilla lalla tilla lalla
Tilla lalla tilla lalla
Tilla lalla tilla lalla

....

Tuii tuii tuii tuii   **13**
Tuii tuii tuii tuii
Tee tee tee tee
Tee tee tee tee

....

Tuii tuii tuii tuii
Tuii tuii tuii tuii
Tee tee tee tee
Tee tee tee tee

....

Tatta tatta tuiEe tuiEe   **13**
Tatta tatta tuiEe tuiEe
Tatta tatta tuiEe tuiEe
Tatta tatta tuiEe tuiEe

....

Tilla lalla tilla lalla   **14**
Tilla lalla tilla lalla
Tilla lalla tilla lalla
Tilla lalla tilla lalla

....

Tuii tuii tuii tuii   **13**
Tuii tuii tuii tuii
Tee tee tee tee
Tee tee tee tee

....

Tuii tuii tuii tuii
Tuii tuii tuii tuii
Tee tee tee tee
Tee tee tee tee

....

Ooo bee ooo bee		6
Ooo bee ooo bee		
Ooo bee ooo bee		
Ooo bee ooo bee		

(*recapitulate the fourth movement from its opening to here*)	(R)	(S)	

development:	(T)	6/1
Ooobee tatta tuu		
Ooobee tatta tuu		
Ooobee tatta tuii Ee		
Ooobee tatta tuii Ee		
Ooobee tatta tuiiEe tuiiEe		
Ooobee tatta tuiiEe tuiiEe		

Tatta tatta tuiiEe tuiiEe   13
Tatta tatta tuiiEe tuiiEe

Lümpff tümpff trill   13
Ziiuu lenn trill   3
Ziiuu lenn trill
Rrumpff tilff too   4

Rinnze kette bee   3
Rinnze kette bee
Rinnze kette bee bee
Rinnze kette bee bee
Rinnze kette beebee beebee
Rinnze kette beebee beebee

Rinnzekete beebee nnzkrr müü?   3
Ziiuu ennze ziiu rinnzkrrmüü
Rakete bee bee   3a

Grimme glimme gnimme bimme   11
Grimme glimme gnimme bimme
Grimme glimme gnimme bimme
Grimme glimme gnimme bimme

Graaaaa | 15
Graaaaa

Grimme glimme gnimme bimme | 11
Grimme glimme gnimme bimme
Grimme glimme gnimme bimme
Grimme glimme gnimme bimme

Graaaaa | 15
Graaaaa

Ooobee tatta tee | 6/13
Ooobee tatta tee
Ooobee tatta tee tee
Ooobee tatta tee tee
Ooobee tatta teetee teetee
Ooobee tatta teetee teetee
Ooobee tatta teeta tatta
Ooobee tatta teeta tatta

Tatta tatta teeta tatta
Tatta tatta teeta tatta | 13

Ooobee tatta tuu | 6/13
Ooobee tatta tuu
Ooobee tatta tuii Ee
Ooobee tatta tuii Ee
Ooobee tatta tuiiEe tuiiEe
Ooobee tatta tuiiEe tuiiEe

Tatta tatta tuiiEe tuiiEe | 13
Tatta tatta tuiiEe tuiiEe

Tilla lalla tilla lalla | 14
Tilla lalla tilla lalla

Tuii tuii tuii tuii | 13
Tuii tuii tuii tuii
Tee tee tee tee

Tee tee tee tee
Tuii tuii tuii tuii
Tuii tuii tuii tuii
Tee tee tee tee
Tee tee tee tee

Ooo bee ooo bee 6
Ooo bee ooo bee
Ooo bee ooo bee
Ooo bee oooobee tatta

Grimme glimme gnimme bimme 11
Grimme glimme gnimme bimme
Grimme glimme gnimme bimme
Grimme glimme gnimme bimme

Tilla loola luula loola 12
Tilla loola luula loola

Grimme glimme gnimme bimme 11
Grimme glimme gnimme bimme
Grimme glimme gnimme bimme
Grimme glimme gnimme bimme

Tilla luula loola luula 12
Tilla luula loola luula

Loola luula loola luula 12
Loola luula loola luula
Luula loola luula loola
Luula loola luula loola

Luula luula luula luula
Loola loola loola loola
Loola loola loola loola
Luula luula luula luula

Ooobee tatta tuu 6/13
Ooobee tatta tuu

Ooobee tatta tuuta tatta
Ooobee tatta tuuta tatta

Tatta tatta tuuta tatta   **13**
Tatta tatta tuuta tatta
Tatta tatta tatta tatta
Tatta tatta taata tatta

Rinnze kette bee   **3**
Rinnze kette bee
Rinnze kette bee bee
Rinnze kette bee bee
Rinnze kette beebee beebee
Rinnze kette beebee beebee

Beebee beebee beebee beebee   **3**
Beebee beebee beebee beebee

Tatta tatta tatta tatta
Tatta tatta tatta tatta

Grimme glimme gnimme bimme   **11**
Grimme glimme gnimme bimme

Graaaaa   graaaaa   **15**
Graaaaa   graaaaa

Lümpff tümpff trill   **10**
Ziiuu lenn trill   **3**
Ziiuu lenn trill
Rrumpff tilff too   **4**

EkeEke ekeEke ekeEke ekeEke   **16**
EkeEke ekeEke ekeEke ekeEke   **16/4**
EkeEke ekeEke Rrrumm!
EkeEke ekeEke Rrrumm!
EkeEke ekeEke Rrum Rrum
EkeEke ekeEke Rrum Rrum

Rrum Rrum Rrum Rrum ……4
Rrum Rrum Rrum Rrum

variation:	**(U)**

Grimm glimm gnimm bimbimm ……11
Grimm glimm gnimm bimbimm
Grimm glimm gnimm bimbimm
Grimm glimm gnimm bimbimm
Grimm glimm gnimm bimbimm
Grimm glimm gnimm bimbimm
Grimm glimm gnimm bimbimm
Grimm glimm gnimm bimbimm

Bumm bimbimm   bamm bimbimm ……11
Bumm bimbimm   bamm bimbimm
Bumm bimbimm   bamm bimbimm
Bumm bimbimm   bamm bimbimm

Grimm glimm gnimm bimbimm ……11
Grimm glimm gnimm bimbimm
Grimm glimm gnimm bimbimm
Grimm glimm gnimm bimbimm

Bumm bimbimm   bamm bimbimm ……11
Bumm bimbimm   bamm bimbimm
Bumm bimbimm   bamm bimbimm
Bumm bimbimm   bamm bimbimm

Bemm   bemm ……11
Bemm   bemm
Bemm   bemm
Bemm   bemm

Tilla loola luula loola ……12
Tilla lulla loola luula
Tilla loola luula loola
Tilla luula loola luula

Grimm glimm gnimm bimbimm (*starts very vigorously*) | 11
Grimm glimm gnimm bimbimm
Grimm glimm gnimm bimbimm
Grimm glimm gnimm bimbimm
Grimm glimm gnimm bimbimm
Grimm glimm gnimm bimbimm
Grimm glimm gnimm bimbimm
Grimm glimm gnimm bimbimm

Bumm bimbimm   bamm bimbimm | 11
Bumm bimbimm   bamm bimbimm
Bumm bimbimm   bamm bimbimm
Bumm bimbimm   bamm bimbimm

Bemm   bemm | 11
Bemm   bemm
Bemm   bemm
Bemm   bemm

cadenza (*ad libitum*) (*here room is left for the cadenza. in performance the cadenza can be recomposed from parts of the sonata as a whole. for now I provide a specimen cadenza using all new themes*)

Priimittii   (V) | 17
Priimiititti

Priimiititti too | 17
Priimiititti taa
Priimiititti too
Priimiititti taa

Priimiititti tootaa | 17a
Priimiititti tootaa
Priimiititti tuutaa
Priimiititti tuutaa

Priimiititti tootaatuu | 17a
Priimiititti tootaatuu

Priimiititti tuutaatoo
Priimiititti tuutaatoo

Tatta tatta tuutaa too   13/17a
Tatta tatta tuutaa too

Tatta tatta tuiiEe tuiiEe   (W)
Tatta tatta tuiiEe tuiiEe
Tatta tatta tuiiEe tuiiEe
Tatta tatta tuiiEe tuiiEe

Tilla lalla tilla lalla   13
Tilla lalla tilla lalla
Tilla lalla tilla lalla
Tilla lalla tilla lalla

Tuii tuii tuii tuii   14
Tuii tuii tuii tuii
Tee tee tee tee
Tee tee tee tee

Tuii tuii tuii tuii
Tuii tuii tuii tuii
Tee tee tee tee
Tee tee tee tee

Tatta tatta tuiiEe tuiiEe   13
Tatta tatta tuiiEe tuiiEe
Tatta tatta tuiiEe tuiiEe
Tatta tatta tuiiEe tuiiEe

Tilla lalla tilla lalla   14
Tilla lalla tilla lalla
Tilla lalla tilla lalla
Tilla lalla tilla lalla

Tuii tuii tuii tuii   13
Tuii tuii tuii tuii

Tee tee tee tee
Tee tee tee tee
....
Tuii tuii tuii tuii
Tuii tuii tuii tuii
Tee tee tee tee
Tee tee tee tee

Ooo bee ooo bee   6
Ooo bee ooo bee
Ooo bee ooo bee
Ooo bee ooo bee

Oooooooooooooooooooooooooooooooo   (X)   6

Dll Rrrrr bee bö   1

Fümms bö wö tää zää Uu,   5
        pögiff,
           müü

Rakete rinzekete   ü3
Rakete rinzekete   3 a
Rakete rinzekete
Rakete rinzekete
Rakete rinzekete
Rakete rinzekete

Bee   1
    bö
Böwö
    böwörö
Böwöböpö
    böwöröböpö
Böwörötääböpö
    böwörötääböpö
    tääböpö
        tüüböpö

    tääböpö
        tüüböpö

Ooka ooka ooka ooka		8
Züüka züüka züüka züüka		9
Rmmp rnnf rmmp rnnf		4
Rumpftillfftoo?	Rrrrrum!	4
Lanke trr gll?	Rrrrrum!	III
Dedesnn nn rrrr?	Rrrrrum!	2
Mpiff tillff too?	Rrrrrum!	2
Zikete bee bee?	Rrrrrum!	3
Fö?	Rrrrrum!	1
Ennze, ennze?	Rrrrrum!	3
Rrumpfftilffto?		4
Bee bee bee bee bee		3a
Zee zee zee zee zee		
Pe pe pe pe pe		8
Pii pii pii pii pii		9
Poo poo poo poo poooo?		
Grimm glimm gnimm bimbimm (*with strong accentuation*)		11
Grimm glimm gnimm bimbimm		
Grimm glimm gnimm bimbimm		
Grimm glimm gnimm bimbimm		
Grimm glimm gnimm bimbimm		
Grimm glimm gnimm bimbimm		
Grimm glimm gnimm bimbimm		
Grimm glimm gnimm bimbimm		
Ooo	bee (*very strong diminuendo*)	6
Ooo	bee	
Ooo	bee	
Ooo	bee	

finale:

Zätt üpsiilon iks (*animated*) (Y) 18
Wee fau Uu
Tee äss ärr kuu
Pee Oo änn ämm
Ell kaa Ii haa
Gee äff Ee dee zee beee?

Zätt üpsiilon iks (*more animated*) 18
Wee fau Uu
Tee äss ärr kuu
Pee Oo änn ämm
Ell kaa Ii haa
Gee äff Ee dee zee beee?

Zätt üpsiilon iks (*simply*) 18 a
Wee fau Uu
Tee äss ärr kuu
Pee Oo änn ämm
Ell kaa Ii haa
Gee äff Ee dee zee bee Aaaaa.

Zätt (*very animated*) (Z) 18
    üpsiilon iks
Wee fau Uu
Tee äss ärr kuu
Pee Oo änn ämm
Ell kaa Ii haa
Gee äff Eeee dee zee beeee? (*dolefully*)

[Schwitters' own directions regarding the "Ur Sonata" can be found in the essay "My Sonata in Primal Sounds" on page 233.]

1923   **Indecent i-Poem**

        Dames-Hemden ....
        Dames-Pantalons, fransch model ..
        Dames-Pantalons ....
        Prima Dames Nachtponnen ......
        Dames-Combinations ....
        Heeren Hemden, zwaar graslinnen

    [Found poem, in Dutch]

circa 1923   **ppppppppp**
        pornographic **i**-poem

        The go |
        Its bleating is |
        Sweet & peaceful |
        And it will not |
        With its horns |

    The black line shows where I cut lengthwise into a harmless poem in a children's picture book. From the goat I got the go.

        And it will not | be provoked
        With its horns | to shove & poke.

    JR

1923   **Banalities (1)**

DADA est une promenade.

> Le Cubisme est une procession.   (Jean Cocteau.)
> Je n'ai jamais pu que mettre de l'eau dans mon eau.   (Fr. Picabia.)
> Le passé et la pensée n'existent pas.   (R. Duncan.)
> Profitez du beau temps pour dormir.   (Anonyme.)

Comment vous applez-vous? Moi aussi.   (Ph. Soupault.)

Prenez garde à l'idéal.   (Anonyme.)

L'art n'est qu'une viande molle et froide. Les cubistes se nourrissent de cette viande. (Fr. Picabia.)

Il n'y aura jamais de faux Dada.   (P. Eluard.)

APRÈS NOUS LA BLENNORRAGIE.   (Docteur Serner.)

When a fiddle's a bit warmed up, it works better.   (Schneider.)

A picture's a map.   (Patsch.)

Willem, you there already? (Fritz.) 'm sorry, no time. (Willem.) Yer just too stupid, Willem. (Fr.) Cause I haven't got the time. (W.) You hypocrite! (Fr.) Cause I haven't got the time. (W.) Well, Willem, it was just as quiet yesterday. (Fr.) Wait till tomorrow then. (W.) Come on, you're nuts. (Fr.) A ripoff artist. Yeah, you are right. (W.) You gonna go nuts too, ya know? (Fr.) My brother-in-law Karl, they had him in the loony bin in Ilten. (W.) You sure make sentences! (Fr.) I can deal with anything. (W.) That's just the way some people do it. (Fr.) Yeah Fritz, that's it. (W.) I think you're just a little ticked off, creep! (Fr.) You really get to me with stuff like that. (W.) You're just a big mouth, there ain't nothing you won't say. (Fr.) Fritz, not another word out of you. (W.)

If you wanna control a horse, you really need to stoke your poke.   (Schneider.)

Lordy Lord, give me your *Sturm*.   (Meidner.)

Don't laugh or you'll get such a whopper your nose is gonna fly straight through the table.   (Mann.)

O Lord our Father, you are sinking a fiery stone ur-deep into the inmost being of this youth.   (Meidner.)

I wanna show you some art for a change.   (Bebbing.)

Lord God, please accept my thanks on my STAMMERING KNEES.   (Meidner.)

Do you know what art is? **Art** is a **SERIAL SHITHOUSE.**   (Bebbing.)

O that I may walk with THEE, with THY Grace, O God, tenderly roofed, springily warmed, and that the o'ercast sky above me ne'er turn bald and TONELESS! (Meidner.)

And on top of it all he shits on me later on.   (Bebbing.)
There have always been young people.   (Kasimir Edschmidt.)

Don't ask such stupid questions!   (Peters.)

Banalities (2)

Lordy Lord, give me your *Sturm*!
Phillip küsste sie und hielt ihre warme Wange gegen die seine für einen Augenblick.* Must always enjoy the present.   (Goethe.)
Now I got to go back into that shit.   (Frontline soldier on furlough in 1917.)
Love is not having something and trying to look for it in someone else. (Fricke.)
But at his most attuned.   (Complete verse by Geibel.)
You can't steal one iota from a word.   (Goethe.)
How much is past.   (Platen.)
If you hold your tongue what flies out from your mouth will never be a bird.   (E. M. Arndt.)
And he who owns it has to be armed for action.   (Goethe.)

SON, HIT   (Stollberg.)

The good man can but be patient.   (Schefer.)
My heart's completely like the sea.   (H. Heine.)
And it was nobody less that Oldman Jahn himself who with a light hand sowed the seed grains for the training of our youth in school and home.   (Anonym.)
For unjust Goodness will not grace our days, and best he is **who gives the great no praise.** (Anonym.) That's the fourth corpse now since February. Like I'm fond of saying: "When it rains it pours." (Our cleaning lady.) Lächeln, Gnädige Frau, immer zu lächeln.*
The dumbest one isn't dumb enough.   (Bodenstedt.)
It doesn't matter if you do a little or a lot.   (Bauernfeld.)
Let young wenches live.   (Old inscription.)
So rarely does that moment come in life.   (Schiller.)
He who can enjoy dry bread will live a happy life.   (B. Reinik.)
10 Feb. 1901 Councillor v. Pettendorff† in Munich   (Obit.)

*[Original text in English]

Don't oase with deserts.   (Nebel.)
BRILLIANTINE is for your hair.
dada makes you crazy without disrupting your career.
In arte voluptas.
It is better to let the storm sweep you into the first available harbor. (Lessing.)

> Laß ruhig fließen
> Im Regen Lauf
> Der Tränen sprießen
> Die Blumen auf.   (Chr. Rellis. trans. K. S.)

Poor Germany! — If it only had Merz!

PJ

Hannover Merzbau: Merz-column, photographed c.1923.
Estate of Kurt Schwitters/VAGA, New York 1991

1923
    1 7 10
    2 7 9
    3 7 8
    4 7 7
    5 7 6
    – – –
    5 8 5
    4 1 4
      –
    3 9 3
    2   2
    1 $\frac{1}{10}$ 1
    2
    3 $\frac{1}{11}$
    4
    5 $\frac{1}{\ }$
    6
    –
    6
    5
    4
    3
    2 Merz 1:2:2:3:4:4:

circa 1926   **Ideas for Poems**

Society for Purposeful Services   / /   Sickness through Health Infinitude

I'm lying in bed, I'm sleeping, flat on my back. A thin sheet of paper. Pressed flat. An other world orbits around me. I'm looking around. That's me there beside me. Or is it? A thin sheet of paper, pressed flat? And your hands? Is it me? Is he you?

It's a carapace lying beside me, empty. Who am I? Is it me there beside me? Not me wrapped up in the covers?: thin cover asleep on my bed: I wake up. Empty carapace. Thin, flat, lies beside me, and sleeps.

*The Wager   The Poet in Overcoat   Greppin
Love under the Oranges*

Andy: Doesn't hardly have eyes, just horn-rimmed glasses, doesn't hardly have teeth, mouth grins from ear to ear. A long thin nose, a wide open nose you'd like to grab hold of. He loves all the little girls. Stands out there dripping.

Stuobanrut

That good Birgenhund hounddog is Hindenburg turned inside out. He got voted in by millions of choice hinds who choose up sides. Choice hinds who choose up sides to have their feelings satisfied. He's the most unlovesome soul in the whole of Germany, because he sees so perfectly. Still there's nothing in his eye, ay, ay, even as the soldier of the nation. But outside the country, my, how they do love him to the sky. Bulldog Birgenhund has got no Easter message for the German folk, his life's completely fuzzy for the whole world not to see. Therefore we cannot talk about him even here: just that he never war no soldier, only a tricky diplomat.

JR

1926–1927   **Autumn / The Last Fly**

Autumn has come, and the curtains are empty.
The flies are departing for the summery south.
Autumn has come, and the curtains are empty.
A pair of orphaned flyspecks on the eyeglasses by the lamp
do still recall the idyll from some golden bygone time.
Autumn has come, and the curtains are empty.
Only a single last fly does sing me its song.
It has much to do, for it has to provide the
illusion of the summery noise of the legions of summery flies.
Little fly,
my sweets,
play roundabout my nose now with your prodigal chirping,
buzz about my dreamy and forever ticklish ear,
that again it may be summer.
Oh you divine last fly,
now you even sit down on the tip of my nose.
Hail thee!
Do sit, my sweet,
get warm,
for the cold season has begun.
Lick off the breadcrumbs on my nose,
till you are quite satisfied,
for I owe it to you that you remind me of summer.

JR [roman] / KS [italic]

1928   **Four Bear Songs**

    1
    Turn this way and that way
    Bear got to spin around.
    Turn this way and that way,
    When he wants a candy treat.
    Then the ladies come in their red hats,
    Then the children come and bawl out loud,
    Then the gentlemen and the ladies laugh,
    Then they say Bravo and they clap their hands,
    And call for an encore and toss him a sweet.
    But the bear won't even pick it up,
    Because he won't even dance for them,
    He'll only dance for a lady bear,
    For the one he loves and has never met.

    2
    So who should the bear love after all?
    The beautiful ladies who look all polished and yummy?
    The sweet young thing who wiggles her tummy?
    Not one of them could endure my love.
    Then where is the Bear Lady whom I could love?
    Where are you hiding the Bear Lady from me?
    When I find her, watch out all those who bother me,
    And tough luck for the woman I happen to love,
    Because bears love to bite when they're making love.

    3
    How whacky is the bear, oh wow!
    There do graze the sheep,
    There does splash the water,
    There do rush the fish,
    There does dance the bear.
    There do flash the rifles,
    There does show his teeth.
    There does smash the table,
    There the bear does choke.
    How whacky is his dance, oh wow!

4
Round about the yellow bearcage
Stands a wall of concrete made.
At its front are iron bars,
Above, a glimmer of blue sky.
The young girls stand on balconies.
They call out "Little Bear, dance, dance,"
We'll give him sugar, fruit, and bread,
See how he waves his funny arms,
But up here we are safe from harm,
The brown bear dances till he's dead.
And over there the hills are big,
The mountain goats are clambering.
They share the hills with the mountain sheep,
With whom they lie down together and sleep,
Because the sheep are too dumb for clambering.
In the restaurant the band toots up.
They play live music three times a week.
And there's also lots of sugar to spare,
Because people don't care if they eat it or not,
So they bring it with them after their coffee.
They get the bear to dance for his sugar
And don't bring anything back to the restaurant.
"Dance for your sugar, dance, little bear, dance.
Here's a little lump of sugar.
That's enough to make you dance."
Then early in the morning comes the bear's deliverance,
The bars fallen down and the bear set free,
He enters on a whole new society,
Picks up culture and good manners to spare,
And like any freeborn person, continues to be the bear.

JR

[*Tortrtalt*], 1929. Collage, 4 x 4¾ in. (10 x 12.2 cm.).
Marlborough Fine Art Ltd., London.
© Estate of Kurt Schwitters/VAGA, New York 1991

1930–1935 **Devil in Need**

In his need the devil does feed on flies.
—So what's new?
Is there something at all he should maybe *not* eat?
Like he didn't have anything better!
I would also myself feed on flies in my need.
—Do you think so?
Like there wasn't even a question.
Well yer don't haveter make such a thing out of it.
Weird devil anyway.
I myself would not feed on flies in my need.
Well feed and let feed.
But you mustn't let other folks feed.
To eat on your own makes you fatter.
Better in need to eat on your own than let other folks feed.
In his need does the devil get fat?
Now I know wherefore I now get fat!
Because the devil in need does feed on his own.
Instead of letting other folks eat.
Flies have short legs.
Lies make you fat.
With only one leg you fly badly.
So who has no flies?

JR

1931   **For Anne: A Poem to Be Sung as a Round**

requiring a good, trivial composition with a very easy to learn
   melody

 O for a good *man*
(the word "good" is to be replaced in the following lines
by, e.g., big—goodlooking—new—strong—brave—rich—
loving—etcetera . . . the inserted words will be performed
in the same sequence by a second singer)
 Cries Anne.
And if he's not so much to start
She loves him soon with all her heart.
He is the man,
He is the man,
Whom she can trust,
She can, she can.
  (At the end the only words are:)
O for a man
Cries Anne.

JR

1935   **If I Were, When I Was**

Untimely gropes without space   The I in the Everywhere You From Morning-Evening-Evening-Morning   toward the next self-consciousness.
From the eternally Old it came,   As I; .   Always growing without degree or measure   It remains in the I.
Soon smaller- larger, up- back   In the You the I, in the I the You   You are like I,   Your I you are,   Like I.
Thus we travel in the Nothing   Unevenly different and differently the same   Uneven evenness (Variable parable) of the millions   Me-Thee, Thee Me: the same way.   Always believing everyone fulfills his duty,   Always faithful to the call within;   The hope that we may unite ourselves,   Remains unsevered.   We live, because we can remember,   And go on living, because we hope.   Time is change all around us,   Space is Cover.
We are the measure,   For Time and eternally,   infinite Space.
We grope, because we know,   If we were, when we were.

PJ

[*Mai 191*], c.1921. Collage, 8½ x 6¾ in.
(21.6 x 17.1 cm.). Marlborough
Fine Art Ltd., London. © Estate of Kurt
Schwitters/VAGA, New York 1991

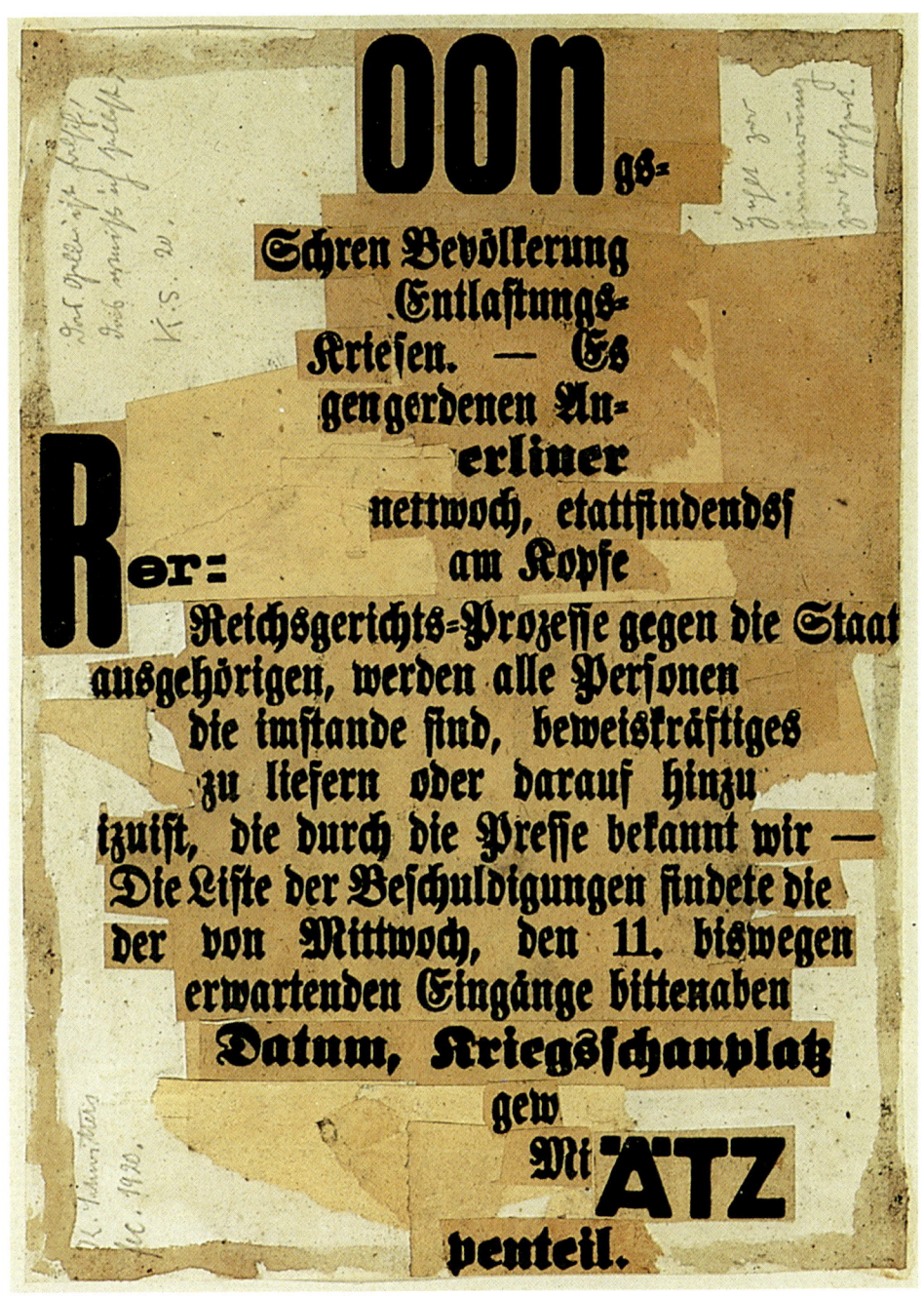

OON [fec], 1920. Collage of cut-and-pasted printed papers, 9⅞ x 7¼ in. (25.1 x 18.2 cm.). Collection, The Museum of Modern Art, New York. Gift of Marlborough Gerson Gallery, Inc. © Estate of Kurt Schwitters/VAGA, New York 1991

[*Difficult*], c.1942–1943. Collage, 31¼ x 24 in. (79.5 x 61 cm.). Albright-Knox Gallery, Buffalo, New York. Gift of The Seymour H. Knox Foundation, Inc., 1965. © Estate of Kurt Schwitters/VAGA, New York 1991

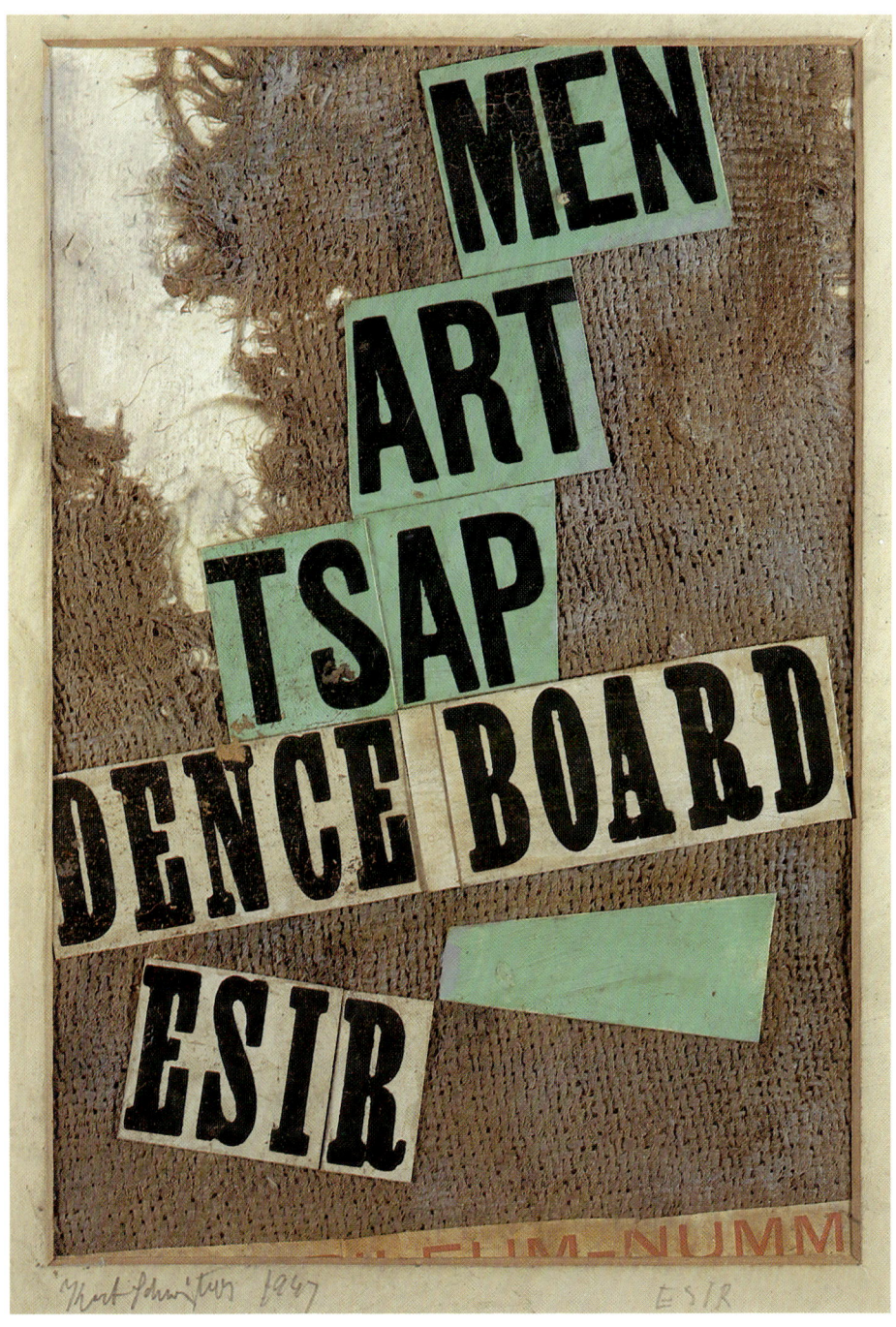

ESIR, 1947. Collage on board, 9½ x 6½ in. (24.2 x 16.5 cm.). Marlborough Fine Art Ltd., London. © Estate of Kurt Schwitters/VAGA, New York 1991

1937   **Premonitions**

When you get old, even the kids make better poems than you, your kids included.

A concrete pigeon in the hand is worth two abstract sparrows on the roof.

Translators' Variation No. 1

A stable pigeon in the hand is worth two flighty sparrows on the roof.

Translator's Variation No. 2

A hard pigeon in the hand is worth two flabby sparrows in the bush.

JR / PJ

1937   **When someone once said**

When someone once said
that some friend had once said
that some other friend said
that I said to a third friend
that a fourth friend had said
that a fifth friend had said
that a sixth friend had said
that I once must have said
what I never once said
let him say for a fact to all those friends
that I now have said
that there was nothing I said.

JR

1937

Small Chinese Poem

I stood before my iron front door.
My friend drove by on a dirigible bicycle.
Then my thoughts remembered her.

PJ

circa 1940

Flight

The Germans are coming—
The Germans?
Here in Norway?
30 bombers flying over—
Is it war?
The airplane down in flames—
Woods burning—
A machine gun—
Radio? So soon?
They've taken Bergen, Trondheim—
Aalesund?
Still free—
And Narvik?
What do the Germans want here?
To help Norway—
Got to pack our things—
Everyone into the cellar—
Got to pack—
You've got to go into the cellar—
Packing—
Too damn dangerous—
What is this life about?
Into the cellar—
No, to freedom.
Where?
Where?

Anywhere but here—
Did you see the airplane burning?
Dogfight over Oslo—
War all right—
That started it—
Attacking a free country—
They just want to help—
No, I don't get it—
We've got to start in packing—
Take just what you need!
Did you hear the machine gun?
Don't leave out your toothbrush—
And the paints—
I'm taking something I can paint with—
They'll be out again soon—
England's helping—
You won't get a chance to paint—
Pack real good—
That lovely freshly painted floor!—
We can't clean up here any more—
They'll be here any time now—
The shooting's ended out in Fornebu—
The wounded are down at the hotel—
We better get a move on—
Pay the the 2 months rent up front!
Go easy, Herr Jensen, you've got no cause to worry—
Well, just don't look back!
We'll be back here in 8 days—
There's no car to be had—
All cars are being used for the evacuation—
Not something you could lend us?—
Take our wheelbarrow!
That gunfire's something awful—
Hurry up, they're shooting from the airplanes!
I'll be going back and forth—
When you get back, we'll have some coffee—
With all of those machine guns—
Hope it goes real well, Frau Jensen!

See you soon, goodbye, take care!
I'll get the wheelbarrow at the station—
They're shooting at us from the airplanes!
Put the bags under the roof!
There, there in the wall, the bullets are hitting—
Here comes the airplane a third time!
No real damage—
But the train looks jammed!
We must be out of their line of fire—
How calm the fjord is in the snow—
Good the three of us are here together—
Tomorrow would have been too late for Esther—
We'll take an auto to the east bahnhof—
No more autos!
Streetcar isn't running—
Electricity's cut off—
We can't carry all this luggage!
Should have filled our papers out beforehand!
Didn't have the time—
What if our records are destroyed?
We ought to stop a passing auto!
There's one coming now!
It's all of the people from the station!
I know a side door there: "Off Limits"!—
If you just know how to go about it . . .
Or else we wouldn't have gotten to the platform—
Good thing the train is running late.
Here it comes now!
Beg your pardon, did I bump you?
There's my third suitcase over there!— —Oh thanks.
Won't you let the old lady sit down?
Oh sure.
Here comes a woman with a baby!
Give her your seat!— — —
Air raid siren.
Well it's finally gotten going!—
Did you see the soldiers in the woods there?
And the snow!

I can still get another postcard off to Helma.
It'll get through.

JR

circa 1942   **Perhaps Strange**

The world is full of goods trains
The passengers are cows
And milk and butter.
And cheese and lovely marmelade
And bulls and horses,
And cocks and hens.
The cow is mother to the milk,
And grandma both to cheese and butter.
The cheese is cousin to the marmalade.
The horse is cousin to the cock
The hen lays eggs.
The egg is cousin to the cheese and butter,
The son and daughter of the milk.
Isn't it strange?
It is.

1942   **There was a little Kew**

There was a little Kew.
The Kew was who?

Hoo Hoo!

You dip it in the water
After all a bath in the nude.
And not so rude.
It went out later
Out of the water
Later and later,
The Kew,
See you later,
Little Kew.

Hoo Hoo.
How do you do?

It does not matter!
The water?
Or the weather?
Why should it matter?
A letter?
A bit of leather?
A Kew from leather!
That is better.
Rather!
I am the father!
With a small letter
For the Kew.

There are a few.
For you!

How do you do?

circa 1942　　**Imagination**

　　　　　　　Four navvies sat on a roof.
　　　　　　　The first one said: "Ouf!"
　　　　　　　The second: "How is it possible then,"
　　　　　　　The third: "That the roof can support us, when—"
　　　　　　　The fourth: "Roofs without girders never can!"
　　　　　　　And then it rang;
　　　　　　　The roof went bang.
　　　　　　　You see!———————

circa 1942　　**Funeral Furnitures at your service**

　　　　　　　Funeral Furnitures at your service
　　　　　　　day and night.—
　　　　　　　Have you see the famous and the infamous?
　　　　　　　Players please.—
　　　　　　　Please keep clear of the dogs.—
　　　　　　　Womans own.—
　　　　　　　Gentlemans own.—
　　　　　　　Hamersmith train—
　　　　　　　Edgware Road—
　　　　　　　Hammersmith train—
　　　　　　　you can rely on asthma—
　　　　　　　high class butcher—
　　　　　　　Bridge clothes cleaning company—
　　　　　　　mist—
　　　　　　　chemist—
　　　　　　　cash chemist—
　　　　　　　cash miest—

1944   **She Dolls with Dollies**

The dollies doll with little dollies,
The little dollies doll with tiny dollies,
The tiny dollies doll with dolly dolls,
The dolly dolls doll with little dolly dolls,
The little dolly dolls doll with tiny dolly dolls,
The tiny dolly dolls doll,
But no one dollies with she.
O thou my darling dolly,
I get to feel so jolly
When I do press my muzzle
Against your guzz—and guzzle.
Dolly jolly
Jolly dolly
Dolly guzzy.
Guzzly dolly dolly lady
First they muzzle then they guzzle.

JR

1945   **Königsberger Is Like That**

If Königsberger says, he pays, then he pays.
Even if Königsberger would not specially say,
he pays, he pays nevertheless.
And if Königsberger pays, he would not say a word.
Königsberger is like that.
And Königsberger would not dare to offend anybody,
because he is rich, and Königsberger is poor.
Königsberger is like that.
When Königsberger pays, he pays, you understand,
but when anybody is rich, you understand?
Therefore Königsberger does not pay.

1945–1947   **Dadar**

At ten past three
Spring ceases to be
All flies that yet here are
All mothers that mammies are
All masters that daddies are
sing songs that dada are
All birds are
Dadar.

1946   **I and You**

I am the bak,
I chissel lak,
I griffel taaler,
I am the Maaler.

You are feudinn,
You chissel tinn,
You griffel turkey,
You are the purkey.

1946

Frohe Tage
London Symphony

HALT
We are specialists!

To be sold to be let
Apply first floor.

High class clothiers
Middle class plumbers
Low class hairdressers
Artistic plumber
Art
Enough said
We save you money
MONEY!

Monarch hair dressing
Dressing gowns
Hairdressing gowns
Gentlemans hairdressing
Gentlemans clothier
Low class hairdressing gowns
Apply second floor!

A B C D

Apply third floor!
Apply within
Apply without
Without hairdressing gown
E F G H I

Apply fourth floor

Preston Preston Preston Bank
A bank in Preston

The power of beef
A bank in Preston
The power of rost beef

Riverside 1698
What do you want?
John Preston
Dig for victory
Without dressing gown
Sell as your waste paper
Rags and metals
Any rags any bones any bottles today?
Milk bar
The same old question in the same old way
All kinds of tools
Fools of all kinds
Ales of all kinds
Allways something to eat
Monday to Friday

In a raid
For coughs for colds
For comfort
For active men
Light refreshments
Rommel tries to cut the net
Underground
Underground station

1946   **And in the night**

And in the night,
When things get round
All corners are round
The darkness is open.
Open in the air.
And the stream
Falls with noise.
When I clap and clap
My trap on your trap.
Pecalamit.

1946   **She is my fairy queen**

She
Is my fairy queen.
Her shoe
Is my fairy shoe.
When I walk on her feet,
It's heaven for me.
I wish from my fairy
Heaven with her.
Round and open
Open through the water.
Open in the air.
Open and round,
Round and open.
Round on one corner.
Who
Understands
You?
And
During the night,
When darkness is open in the air,
All things are round
On all corners.

1946   **Count Sardinowhocount**

In einer Mannsarde
Lebte eine Frau Sarde
Nein, eine Frau Sardine
Hinter der Gardine
Mit ihrem Mann,
Herrn Sardinowhich.
Which Sardinowhich?
Mann Sardinowhich.
The Sardinowhich, which lived in the Herrsarde.
Oh no, the Sardinowho
Who lived in the Mannsarde.
With his wife, Miss Sardine.
Pardon Misses Sardinesse.
C'était une comtesse
Called Madame Sardinesse.
He was a count
Called Mr. Sardinowhocount,
Who counts the amount
Der Mannsarden
Annonciert in der Presse
Mit seiner Fresse.

1946   To avoid
        To avoid
        To avoid
        Zelloloid

1946 **London Onion**
[*Variations about the theme of the Thames valley*]

    I

LONDON
Ell Ou enn De Ou enn.
Ell
Ell Ou
Ell ou enn
Ell Ou enn enn
Ell Ou enn enn
Ell Ou enn enn
Ell Ou enn enn
De Ou enn
Ou enn
enn
enn enn
Ell Ou enn De Ou enn
enn Ou Ell enn Ou De
Ou Ell
Ou De
Ou Ell
Ou De
Wra.
Ou De
Wra
Ou Ell
Tackelamit
Wra
London
Wra

    II

Onion
Opinion
Zegoday
Onion
Opinion
Zegodayda

Onion
Opinion
Zegodaydatoo
Zegodaydataa
Onion
Opinion
Zegodaydatuu
Zegodaydatau
Too taa
Tuu taa
Too taa
Tuu taa
Zegodaytatuutaa
Prrrr!
Tootagrö.
Te tear
U uncle
Agrö
Tootagrö
Tootagrö mesens
Tootagrö mesans
Tootagrö tear
Tootagrö tear mesens
Tootagrö tear mesans
Tootagrö uncle
Tootagrö uncle agrö
Prrrr!
How item King
C Charley
D Dog
L Love
L London
Love London
I love
Dog Charley
I Dog.
Dog Love
I Dog Love London Charley.

Onion
Opinion
Ell Ou Enn De Enn Enn
Ell Ou Enn De Enn Enn
Ell Ou Enn De Err Err
Ell Ou Enn De Err Err
De Ou enn
De Ou enn
Ou enn
enn.
Prrrr.
What is your verdict?
Verdict A
Verdict Be
Verdict A
Verdict Be
Ell.
Oh, my sweetest Toots,
I don't care two hoots,
When I clap and clap
My trap on your trap!
Ell Oh enn De Oh enn.
Zegodayda!
Zegodayda!
Zegodayda!!!

Just in the middle of her knee
There I observed the fact that she,
Possessed a little reddisch mole
It was alone, just one and sole.

And even if there had, may be,
Been two, which were just on her knee,
Just in the middle would be one
      (In fact it does)
A fact that I would beg you to discuss.

Be ll arr Aa enn
Bee

Bee Aa
Bee Aa ar
Bee Aa arr arr
Bee Aa arr arr
Bee Aa arr arr
Bee Aa arr arr
Ell Oh enn enn
Ell Oh enn enn
Ell Oh enn enn
Ell Oh enn enn
De Ou enn
Arr Aa enn
Beran
London
Teckalamit.

1946   **Opinion**

Opinion
Par Avion
Onion opinion
Par Avion
Herbert Read
Naoum Gabo
Tuntagrö
Nelly
My dear friend
Par Avion
I am so glad
Par Avion
Aa vee I ou ennenn
I ou enn
ou enn
enn
London

circa 1946–1947   **One day**

>One day
>You finish to be a boy.
>But you play
>Still with your old toy.
>You like all the old angels
>As you did before,
>And think they are girls,
>Beautiful girls.
>You think they are like you
>When you were young
>But you are old,
>And die and get cold.

circa 1946–1947 **Far away from**

    Far away from
From the noise
On the pretty farm
Of the noise of a battle
From the silence of old poetry
I wait for you
My bony girl, my bonny bony
I wait.
The cocks run on top of the hens
The hens hide under the cars
The soldiers play with trars bars brars
Rhyme comes on rime
That is the art of riming
The waiting makes me old
The waiting makes you bonny bony
Cars sit on top of cars
And lay eggs.
The father car coc
Sits on the mother egg
And makes
And makes
A little tiny tittle
A tiny little car.
It is a male car
And cries
KE KE REE KEEAR

1947 **At first men were limited**

At first men were limited
                limited
                limited,
Until than they imited
                imited
                imitated;
But when than they imited
                imited
                imitated,
Still they remained limited
                limited
                limited.

1947 **The Prisoner**

Shooting not allowed.
Sour saussage towers in itself.
The little violet has an eye with which it
Green little fish cry round about them
A dead body baked together from yellow seagulls.
Eight o'clock Segall is their father and mother. (Express)
Because my wife has a very much salted tongue back on her
    head wigs pale sour cream
Raoul Hausmann breaks softly towered up redamaged wheels
    left from right
Blood boils in streams of uteries before Apollinaire round
    peaks feet mountains
Left and right—left and right—left and right—right and left.
One two, one two, one two, one two,—one!

circa 1947

A fishbone fish a fefishbone

A fishbone fish a fefishbone
Lay on the on lay on the stone.
You may believe the sea has thrown
The fefefishbone there upone.

There came a fish a fefe (whistle) fisher,
A fefefisher came alone.
He used to sit while he was fefishing
He uuused to ssit upon this stone.

The fisher saw while he was fishing
While he was fishing saw the bone.
He took it took he tetetook it,
He tetetook it from the stone.

Now lies the lies now lies the stone
Without a out without a bone
And all surrounded by the water
The pepeparn stone is alone.

1947   **Pin**

A pennhole by phan
The whole PIN by phan
A pinnhole by phant
Phanta
Phantas
Phantasia
　　　Asia
　　　　Europe and
　　　　America.
　　　　　Erica
　　　　　Erica!
A whole thing by Erica
Phanterica . . . Amasia
Amusia
Asia Usia
A thing of phantasia.
The right thing for right phan
The world needs phan.
Phan in phan.
Phan are old tendancies in poetry and paintry,
Phan are new tendancies in poeting and painting
In poeting and Paintry
Phan in Ting and Try
Fun by Phan
Phan leads; the old fun is not any more able to lead further
— — — — — — — — — — — —on.
You cannot get phan if you have not got it.
Pin penns phan.
We have to conquer bombs, we have to conquer rockets;
by phan.
The phan atom bomb conquered by penn phan.
Muses are nomore on holidays.
M a n k i n d   m u s t   s u r v i v e .
We conquer the Atomb by phan

Creative capacities are sunken deep in the very
    wartime. People are crying for spirits:
  f.e. whisky. We devellop by our will, by our
    power creative spirits. We will devellop
    creative spirits. The world shall no more
    be dry. No more.
Listen: We jear with our ears and see with our eyes.
Not with our tongue. Oh no !
Tat are our drils and quadras.
Phan-drils and Phan-dras
Our phantastic quadrills and triquadras are
full of stic. Full of mystic. They encounter the lack
of *w h i s k y* after the war. They will overrun and overwhelm
"modery poetry" which is only "Aufgewärmter Kaffee."
by their superior formel life and character. By negative
expressions.
No negotiations with negative expressions.
NO :
Phan means No Nego.
Their desobjectivised contents are direct.
They are placed above the meanings of language
        at all
The language is only a medium to feel. Not to understand.
Do you understand that ?
You understand ?
Do you really understand ?
Do you understand that there are things which
you cannot understand ?
You understand, it is difficult, not to understand.
Why speak a language which you shall not stand under ?
Why paint a picture which you shall not read ?
Which you cannot understand ?
You reader; you !
You shall become a feeler.
Come, be a good child, give up your human controlled
  feelings,
and PLEASE kreep through our brush, kreep through our
  penn,

kreep through our pennhole, our pinhole our PIN, and you will
know that you dont know anything.

That is the right and that is the left thing of Phan.

1947 **Die Gazelle zittert**

Die Gazelle zittert,
Weil der Löwe brüllt.
Die Hyäne wittert.
Doch die KUNST ERFÜLLT.

The gazelle trembles

The gazelle trembles,
As the lions roar.
The hyena shambles.
But ART GIVES MORE.

PJ

PROSES

&

PLAYS

1919   **The Onion**
        Merzpoem 8

The day that I was to be slaughtered was a very busy day. (Don't be afraid, just keep the faith!) The king was set, his two attendants waiting. The butcher had been asked to come at six thirty; it was a quarter to seven and I gave the orders myself to start the customary preparations. We had picked a spacious hall so that the many spectators could watch the show in comfort. The telephone was near to hand. The doctor was living in the house next door and was on call in the event that any spectators passed out. (A keepsake from your confirmation.) Two powerful tackle blocks were hanging from the ceiling, to crank me up should they decide to gut me. Four strong laborers were there to lend a hand: erstwhile Russian prisoners of war, big-boned and hardy handsome (*Journal for Real Estate and Household Management*). Two well scrubbed maids were also there on call, two super-scrubbdup farmgirls. It was a real kick thinking that these two young girls would whisk my blood and wash and salt my innards.

The hall had been swept and washed. I had two long, cleanscraped tables set up along one of the walls, on which stood several bowls, knives, forks. Now I had a wash basin, water, and a towel brought in, also some dish detergent (Sunlight). Anna and Emma, the two maids, brought out a bucket and a whisk. Knowing that you'll be butchered in ten minutes gives you a funny kind of feeling. (The sacrifices of a mother's love.) Until then I had never in my life been butchered. It takes a lot of growing up. Anyway, once the potatoes have been taken out and once the oats are cut, that's when things can turn real bad. And so far we haven't had a decent summer anyway. (Faith, love, great expectations.) (Ducks are goosing in the meadow.) Every little detail taken care of.

And now the princess was arriving. She had a short white dress on, which had got a little twisted, but that only made her sexier. Because the church tower is extremely steep. Dedicated to Lenzesflur in friendship. Jumping and kicking, the king's daughter and her delicate short legs. I love these delicate kicking jumpingkingsdaughterslittlelegs. Tail waggles sour cream. She herself stood inkwell to my face and whistleclean asked white embroidery. "Are you going to be butchered now today?" Hot fishing knives shot blood. I lowered purple eyes, made happy by her greeting. "How beautiful you are, you Elvis Broomsticker, gorgeous hunk!" she said red lips veins do boil blood, happy trails! pert sharplythreaded nose: "I'm bringing you last greetings from the world. Thou should become a nun! (May my house be thy world.) (Leather without a head.) Tooled leather set to navel measure. These days you're really in a hurry, getting things lined up for this important day. (Peace be with you.) How you do grow up—grow ripe—grow overripe! How joyfully you look at your own ripeness! May it always bring you joy! How lucky that the weather stayed good for your butchering, that way the butcher can get here by bike." (Authentic Brussels handiwork.) Good Health is Fortune's Gift. "Please, little princess, will you let me phone. It is half past six already and the butcher isn't here." "Hello! Is this the butcher speaking? The spectators are starting to get restless, how come you aren't here yet?" (From here yet to eternity!) "Have them start up the festivities without me. I just kebabd my sister on the church spire, like a weathervane. And as you know the church spire is very steep and up above it a fish spikes in whipair. The lightning rod was very rusty and tough to jab it through my sister's belly. But fish spikes blank in whipstink. Have them start up the formalities without me!"

I let the king be called. "Majesty, I do commend my lovely form unto thine hands. May your majesty take command over my corpse-to-be!" (20 cents per millimeter line per six-column page.) The king waved back. (Fortuna Grindstones.) The two attendants in black frockcoats, gloves, top hats, and black neckties, took their places at the king's two sides. A black dog flew past, cawing. Again the king waved. The four Russians plus Anna and Emma got ready to lend a hand. The king waved again. The attendants approached me, stood in front of me, and asked about my last wishes. (Look up at that star!) I requested the princess to sing the great workers song and then kiss me. (Acephalous necks, leather jerky.) A lady from the royal entourage swooned and fell down on the floor. The doctor was summoned. Strong does whip inward. The princess then sang:

"Workers grind organs
"C-sharp D
"D-sharp E-flat
"E-sharp E
"Thou thine thy thee,"
the very great workers song. Lanternstake does grind organ do kiss the broad skirts wave white points a kiss. To sling arms broad skirts do wave neck points warm tubes do smooth slim fish carps, carps, carps. (Prière de fermer la porte.) Please, please close the door, Thou, Thou, Thou! For I love thee so very! (This world with its sinfuls.)

Now butcher me!

The king waves again and the butcher drives forth. The house has gone mute. Pro patria est, dum ludere videmur (blue-red-yellow girls club). (Smoking Forbidden. Even unlit cigars held in hand are prohibited.) Two laborers who took his bike away. (National welfare tax.) A laborer brings out a cudgel, big lemon-pale balloon. (Hold on to what you've got!) The butcher wears a blue striped apron flutter cloth. (Beet Sugar Baby.) October bends down ceremonies enemies attendants.—Scat!—Me hedgehog!—Butcher is leaning back, head tilted, cudgel raised behind. (The greatest gift, the fairest joy, is homesweethome domestic bliss!) The butcher springs forward (That's love for you), swings cudgel down down down hard hard hard, does whip inward down hard hard hard very very very very.

My skull caved in.

Now I had to fall to pieces, so I fell, I fell to pieces, fell, fell flat. Aaaaa aaaaa aaaaa aaaaa b. (Applause from all the benches.)

So what's the story now? They strapped my arms and legs to winches, winches winch me up. Sinking slings flat to pieces slantly spread out. (Calling all blue- and white-collar workers.) They stabbed me in the side. Blood rinseth bucket blue stream red thick whip. Turns maids a whisk to pieces break upon the wheel railroad machines do Emma Anna whisk. (In all innocence you 'ave hallowed thy heart for the Holy Alliance t'day!) The king demanded a drink. Blue singed flame murder far gone far gone. Hollow burns stomach flame sulfur blood. Since which time the king is beardless. Be true to your duty, be true. (Presented by the Editorial Committee.) For everything has its own science. (Amplificatores, Advisory Council for Capitalist Reconstruction, Berlin.)

They were going to gut me. (Newest Mocha Bonbons, A Novelty.) Transfers drive knife do slit tremble intestines. (Peace Commodities.) It was a garden restaurant well worth the visit. I felt a thousand joys o savior morning twenty. The creature bred in the glass house blossomed only for three lustra. (Roaring cheers.) Mooncalf inward glows soft pulled intestines fat pain soft swoond. (All this for the Red Army.) Clean, clean, be clean, girls, clean when washing, so that nothing will get burnt. (May God preserve you.) (God preserve you.)

Flame hot, flame hot! Earthworms inward played soft in my belly, it tickled so slight. The king lusted my eyes. O fetch me, king's daughter, the eyes of Johanan. (Thou art moving this day from the House of thy Father.) Round spheres inward smooth slime they sprang from the eyes the soft hands fully toward. With a plate, knife, and fork they served eyes. (Old warriors hard of hearing and totally deaf get facts and advice at no charge.) Smooth slimed oysters eyes sink stomach heavy. Children under twelve admitted only with parental supervision, children under eight must be led through by hand. (Admission 50 pfennigs, minimum one mark.)

"Poison!" screamed the king while rolling on the floor. (To populate the earth, the cradle proves its worth.) "Sweet dreams, but in the meantime I've been poisoned." (31 days in August, daytime growing shorter by one hour 56 minutes.) You bet, it really sucks. "O Lord I build my house on thee, I raise my hands!" Two mushrooms grew eyes stem smooth tubers milk skyhigh and drilled holes two into king's belly. Stemeyed eyes did eye. Mute scared a king chalk. Princess's heart was beating something awful. (Acetyline eliminates the smell of bodily secretions.) She felt such wondrous pity for her father. The doctor was summoned fussing with the holes in the king's belly. (Veritas Vincit—Anna Blossom in the starring role.) Then the old king passed out. Fear peaks silver tendrils stone to stone. The princess waved and ordered them to put me back together. (That's how one cleans, dusts, washes, steams, and dries bed feathers.)

They started to put me back together. With a little gentle pressure they pushed my eyes back in their sockets. (Have no fear: faith, love, great expectations are thy stars.) Then they gathered up my innards. Happily nothing had been cooked yet, and nothing had been ground up for sausages. (Vaincu, mais non dompté.) And still one is pleased to see another pretty autumn. Because of my inner magnetic currents, my inner parts (once they were stuffed inside) began to jerk spasmodically and then stuck hard and fast together. (The art of happy days in marriage.) When setting the intestines back in place, certain problems had to be worked out, that was how much they'd gotten intermeshed. (Saint Florian Moves into German Theater. Comic Extravaganzas Nightly.) But I noticed what was going on, directed my magnetic currents hither and thither, to and fro, one two one two one two one the tone to uproot mote in eye. I pushed and pulled magnetically on the intestines, until they lay in their accustomed places. My knowledge of man's inner nature was a boon to me. (After a one-year tryout, lands a permanent position as a Prussian state official.) Jawohl! Meanwhile my solid parts had been put back together; the only thing still missing was the blood. (Bordens sweet milkchocolate.) The maids held the bowl with blood under the stabwound in my side and whisked it in the opposite direction. The king gave an audible groan. Drawn by my magnetic currents a thick jet of blood rose up from its red surface and slammed into my stabwound. (Mustn't tell the girls what every woman has to know.) Slowly my veins filled up, my heart was full, the inner parts began to take in blood. But the heart didn't move, I was still dead. (Fresh paint!) With his knife the butcher touched the stabwound in my side, plunged the blade in deep, pulled the knife out—and the wound closed up. (Detach and mail to the above address.) That's why every woman should inform herself, at least once she has gotten married. Once again now all my parts were back together, there were just a few small holes where bits of flesh were still adhering to the knives. The desire and the need for it are clearly present, although the time ain't right. Besides there was a lack of blood, because the king had drunk it. (For the ideals of socialism.) Ever since I've been a tad anemic. Take the cage home with you and buy yourself a bird. The lowered winches winched down tackle blocks. Now I had to straighten up, I thought, and so I straightened up; quickly at first and then slower and slower until I was standing up straight. (My heart and maw were red and raw.) A slip of a girl grew up in Burgundy, for I am only a squaw. O child, be mindful of whither you move! Be faithful and true! Remain faithful, o child, step forward in life, don't be shy. (Vote socialist too!) Then the two attendants took places beside me, ceremoniously grasping my hands. (Prescriptions filled for all health plans.) Beautiful childhood is over and past, the struggle for life has now started at last. And I was dying to know how they would bring me back to life. (Ism-supervisor von Jefim Golycheff.) It is strictly forbidden to touch any object in this collection. I was dizzy. (Strindberg to gradually unroot Stramm.) Our good old teacher liked to spice his teaching up with little jokes, and there was nothing wrong with that. (Sungazing.) I don't believe in anything. (Trumpet jamboree.) You got it right! In this most trying of times an appeal to all Bible-thumping evangelical woman preachers! (What every man should know about pregnancy and childbirth!) Your maw's a saw. (Old Doctor Sunshine.)

The butcher grabbed his cudgel again (the tragedy of being human), stood it in front of me (the behavior of men during pregnancy), and gently rested it on my split skull. (Rudolf Bauer's a genuine artist.) Anna Blossom abideth lilac-blue roses does shoot sting hole stinkhole. (Ripe for the plucking, united at heart.) Incomplete information misses the mark. Then the butcher jumped backward with a godawful jerk. (The major is and will always be a "gentleman," although he's also a twit.) That woman has to know it all. There was a godawful crash when the cudgel drew back from my head. A book designed especially for women offers this rare chance. Table of Contents: 1. How to win love.—2. The tamed shrew.—3. What girls go for in a man.—4. Something about kissing.—5. How to make a good impression.—6. How to deal with a rejection.—7. Is shyness justified in marriage?—8. The roots of abstinence.—9. Older views.—10. How to practice moderation.—11. A good piece of advice.—12. Is love blind?—13. How to recognize true love.—14. The man's past.—15. The most intimate intimacy.—16. The new faith.—17. The dark star. The butcher jumped backward into his original stance. (He shall be your Lord.) But the company's true pillar remains forever without guile. (Jamais embrassé.) The bits and pieces of my skull flew back together, I was just about complete again. (Sweet moment.) Fritters you don't like, and gherkins are too fat for you. And anyway the theater only exists for people who aren't people anyway. The book is richly illustrated and will be sent you on receipt of payment due.

It felt really strange to be alive again. Seltzer water sails light up perfume Maria. I felt I had to pose a little, and so I posed a little. (Just then the king died.) With a grand flourish I walked up to the king's daughter and offered her my hand in silence. (Kiss me!) The king's daughter fell on her pretty bony knees in front of me. (From back in downhome country.) The doctor meanwhile fletcherized pork knuckles. Help wanted ads continued in the supplement. She begged me urgently to save her father. (Happiness inside the haidehaus.) I knew I couldn't stay good-natured in this instance, not when anyone can spot a dummy by his easy nature. (Anna Blossom hanging tough.) (Old age real scary.) I told her: "Your father the king, the king will stay dead." (Razor strap from seal pelts.) Then the doctor swooned. I had them set two candles made of yellow wax into the king's belly, then had the candles lit. (Payment in stamps.) When the flame flared through the holes in the king's belly, the king exploded. But the people offered me a last hurrah. (Socialism = Work.)

PJ/JR

1920   **Kurt Schwitters to the Swiss Dadaist Arp.   Blackberries (2)**

belivered pra!
   first I say why?
why does one use upper case and lower case? i use only lower case. then I say why? why does one punctuate i write everything without punctuation then i ask why why does one use umlauts i won't be straight diacritical henceforth i will write zurich fülfills seclusion personal carryover and then i remember the old phrase from mathematics namely that it does not matter in which order i add respect multiply and now i write vole instead of love because love needs voles to love voles and finally now will giveup the or derofwordsamongthemselvesbywritingonlyonegiantwordorwhilemorewrotitsoladinorthographyisnaturallyunimportantandsenseigiveupinfavorofnonsenseandthustheitsheklmnoppqrsutabelgikemaminopetroleumplaguekakrrkrrksrstopitonobilamenteyakkaanteelinguekitonpausbacrocodilemmadiemadilemma[1])

                                                                    kuwitter

[1]Here the typographer went stark raving mad and threatened a general strike, should he be forced to set any more Kuhgewitter (Cowweather).

PJ

1922	**A Quarter of the Feelings of Old Man Automato in His Ancestral Castle Atho**
A Romance

Atho.
Auto.
Automato.
The dog gawks his schluck on the axis of
Liqueur.
Which of you incited the scraper?
That you dare gawk at me!
Nymphoschematics eye glimmer eyes.
The calf is dead.
On the chicken's rear end stands a ladder.
Streetcars ride back and forth on it.
Wireless.
Poco sonore.
Automatic.
The dog warms the inner field.
When the wild wine blossoms.
My left eye itches.
The calf stays dead.
Bicyclists must keep within the lanes assigned.

JR

1922 **The Secret Drawer**
A Novelette

"We'll never give our permission to do that." "Daddy, I'm 25 years old!" (Complete idiot.) "what you mean by that is: no chance?" (Truly, Else, I pity you!) The magistrate keeps himself ready now as before to lend his electric bell. "And what do you think you'll do?" "Well, papa, let me tell you." "Then there's nothing more I have to say to you." The voice of conscience: "Hail gilded recklessness!" (Rack and field) Leona turned and left the room. The old writing table stood up. (Crooked legs.) Chickenpowder the air from day to day the legs. The whole beach is family bath. Most families that reside here (semplice, sonore.) have however not yet passed the registry. But it also works this way, each shot a mark, for the wingbeat of a free soul wings it sideways into the bushes, as if it wanted to explode from sadness and weariness of life. What is leariness? Moritz Nadir dies.

"Daddy, is that your last word?" "My last word, Leona!" But the old writing table sighs icily, for tactical reasons.

Many go into the water wearing their underwear and let the dear sun do the drying. (Technical term) Trained and raised to their full height they downfaced each other, resembling each other in figure and appearance (emotion.), and more of the same. Victor indulgingly split the sheet in two and wrote cross column-wise: "But I love you so much!"

The writing table remained silent for a moment. (behind.) "And what happened then?" asked the coquettish pillarclock. (otherwise your plasterplait breaks!) to the pure everything is pure, even if it's filthy water. Life is a reform school, registered trademark # 97487. (Schulze clarifies his standpoint for himself.)

Nobody may be laid crosswise over the street; for whose lodgings do not spit in the wagon. (Get yourself away!) 1.) away. 2.) to get. 3) full bath? "And that's all," the clock said contemptuously?

How she trembled the width of longlong hours. Where bathing is the custom, nudity's part of the mores. The dead have no need for heads. (cf. Otto Nebel.) The Baroness Leona was washing the bedroom on her knees, always separated by miles, compassionate, ready to help, lying with word and deed on top of the helpseeker's head. Leona hastily searched through her narrow purse—always indicate what kind—and gave the young man a five pfennig piece. (Berlin has its Wannsee, Rostock its Warnemünde, Lübeck its Travemünde, Hannover its Steinhude.) He put it into an envelope. How happy Leona could be! "Little miss," said the old writing table, "I am very experienced, I have gone through many feet. Many have lain in my secret drawer." (who has unlocked the wells, now birds flow from the cool pipes) "Just think," interjected the baroness, who had stood on the couch, wringing her legs, watching the fight between father and daughter, "a darksquareseamstress, the first tragedy by a shoemaker, a skinflint's last will and testament, funny money, a suicide's farewell letter, on the part of an oily ox, presently he canalizes in journals. Time demands renunciation, having done too much is in the end little. Others have the most modern bathing trunks, elegant like filmstars in the illustrated papers, at times full, with 5 cuffs one over the other, at times empty like flyvelvet. ("Honors replace knowledge.") And then? Then sunshine flooded the room again, and the little woman twittered again in her husband's eyes as she had done earlier. Yes, when one is young, one just can't believe that something like firewood exists.

Then she sat down and wrote first a mean, unforgiving letter, but the spelling was wrong. Oh, those damn foreign words, all the legs are topsy-turvy! In Hannover, just as in Berlin, Rostock, and Lübeck, those saturdays and sundays, when yearning hotly squints, are firstclass bathing days. £136. Habit, piety, and consideration for others had a part in it, and those are the ties that turn man, without the latter noticing it, into a slave. (From the rear that becomes too expensive.) She tore it up and rewrote it, full of spelling mistakes and reproaches for the terrible offenses she is suffering. And thus one schlepps many a thing with one through life et se purifie entièrement au dépôt général en gros.—Verilà.—Voilà.

Those were jolly Christmas days! Nothing but old acquaintances. But then there came a time when the eyes of the little woman became very strange, like crow's eyes or like bunions and then she took up residence under the chair by the window. (A one-act play!) Her knees were trembling and quaking. The bustle of the municipal swimming pools is the best proof. At any rate, she is a good and courageous human being, or else she wouldn't be the friend of His Excellency the Baron.

Many letters she wrote and then tore up. Finally one of them turned out to be calligraphically correct. Your Future Too is in danger. It casts Revon in a bad light (magnesia), that its municipal authority always brings to night an anxious watershyness (*vide* fire department) and still shows it today. Your future too is presently in danger! The number of those who govern is great. For love of the U. S. P. D. they will put it in the street, crosswise. Affliction has turned him into a great artist, it nearly broke me. Your future too is presently in the past! (K. A. P. D. = Kaiserliche ANNA BLUME Partei Deutschlands.)[1] In his imagination the loaded wagons were already rolling along the railroad tracks. Until finally everything she knew was in one letter. Then came the day when for the first time a real secret was hidden in my drawer—a bad, bad, secret. What did this letter conceal? Did it contain the decision of a foreign artist in which she saw the decision that would affect the rest of her life? (Franz Müller drinks shoeliveroil.) Illnesses bring down the body, especially mulled illnesses. The young man brought letters that odored a strong odor and were full of hot, enticing words. (79° Réaumur.) With trembling fingers she opened the letter. Then she sat for a long time, her feet in her lap, as if in a dream. Then she opened her arms wide, and a sort of trance came over her, a breathless boundless joy. (Schnapps is schnapps.) And yet he brought again and again such a sweet-smelling letter, and the eyes of the small woman grew sadder from day to day.

Illnesses get everywhere, as does death. But once she came with red eyes and happy cheeks, like shining gold coins, says Goethe. Acting important she pulled out a red briefcase, into which was stitched a small enchanting basket of roses and delicate forget-me-nots and joyful ribbons. But that too came to an end.

[1] [Translator's note: K.A.P.D. = Kommunistische Arbeiter Partei Deutschlands, or Communist Workers Party of Germany.]

The next day the man looked into the drawer. In it there was a small piece of paper with only these words on it: "Franz Müller's wirespring."

Instructions for use:

Legs 2–5 turn leg 1. The heavy world war is over. Several thousand marks are still missing. But even if the enemy had demanded the dissolution of the legs, the provisioning of the fighters for peace and order would have had to be carried out. You know that I was in love with Erich Findeisen.

I tremble with fear that she may find the mean letters, but she forced the drawer open and, astonished, pulled out the letters. Poor small woman! The fists she made! The reason was finally only the fear of the street. Especially crosswise. Until there suddenly erupted from the ground of her soul, like hiccuped raspberry juice, sourly, an exultant, jubilant hiccuping, the like of which she had never known. Women should take that into consideration. The greatest enemy of many women is lack of knowledge. All night long I had to sigh over these letters. The dead only act as if, and my sighing kept the man from sleeping. The way for it is traced out. Earth drinks water. Man whimpers more.

And with the rays of this joy still in her eyes, Leona went over to her parents.

PJ

1922

Vexation Plays
A Dramatic Sketch

a. Sir:
b. Yes?
a. You are under arrest.
b. No.
a. Sir, you are under arrest.
b. No.
a. Sir, you are under arrest.
b. No.
a. Sir, I'm going to shoot.
b. No.
a. I hate you.
b. No.
a. I will crucify you.
b. Nope.
a. I will poison you.
b. Nope.
a. I will murder you for the sheer pleasure of it.
b. Nope.
a. Just think about winter.
b. Never.
a. I hate you.
b. Never.
a. I kill you.
b. Like I say, never.
a. I am going to shoot.
b. You've already said that once.
a. Please come along now.
b. You cannot put me under arrest.
a. Why not?
b. At best you may detain me.
a. In that case I'll just detain you.
b. Please, go ahead.
b. *lets himself be arrested by a. and is led away. The lights go down on the stage. The public, feeling cheated and wrongly made fun of, boos and whistles.*
The choir screams: Stupid! Poet, ouuuut! What crap!

PJ

1922   **Dramatic Sketch**

MAN   *vomits*
WOMAN   Wipe it up!
MAN   I feel rotten.
WOMAN   Wipe it all up!
MAN   I feel really rotten.
WOMAN   You swine, keep it moving.
MAN   I'm going to vomit.
WOMAN   You're befouling my house.
MAN   I feel really rotten.
WOMAN   I'm going to spit on you.
MAN   I'm going to vomit.
WOMAN   I'll spit in your mouth.
MAN   Hold me tight!
WOMAN   You old slut!
MAN   That makes it feel better.
WOMAN   I'm going to whup you.
MAN   O, you're really so good.
WOMAN   You swine, you porcupine!
MAN   You, you!
WOMAN   Cool it, you camel!
MAN   I'm going to puke.
WOMAN   *beats him* Just hear it purring.
MAN   Ouch.
WOMAN   Just hear it yapping.
MAN   Gracious lady!
WOMAN   Buggrrrr.
MAN   Ouch.

JR

1922   **Buckets**

Today, after long and patient suffering, death came to him (dog-bones brain steamrolls 4-thousand) who was my much loved husband, our dearest father, mother, grandmother, great grandmother, son, and daughter: William the Shipping Clerk Mary the Christine Miss Googles. (Monkey Girl Biker.) Was she not A loyal SALAry man, alwayS in there pitcHing, managing His business to oUr satisFaction. (There's an onIon.) All such asservations, namely that I climbed up in the tree dressed only in a shirt and that I then read, read the typhoon there, are totally untrue.

J R

1922

Extr. #30

AUGUSTA BOLTE
(a liver extract.)

by

KURT MERZ SCHWITTERS

FIFTH PRINTING

1923

Verlag Der Sturm / Berlin

AUGUSTE BOLTE

> dedicated to
> 1. AUGUSTA
> 2. Art criticism
> 3. The Lif faculty,
> 4. All my dear friends.

(a doctoral dissertation)*

The author reserves all rights, especially reproduction, translation, live presentation, and film rights. The author logically performs his own compositions

Motto: Of course one wishes everything good to all people, but the bad happens of itself.

(Doris Thatje)

Poem: O man, do not hurt this one,
      This is no pencil, this is chalk.
      It has the right to think.
      So we won't insult it any further.

*with footnotes

INTRODUCTION

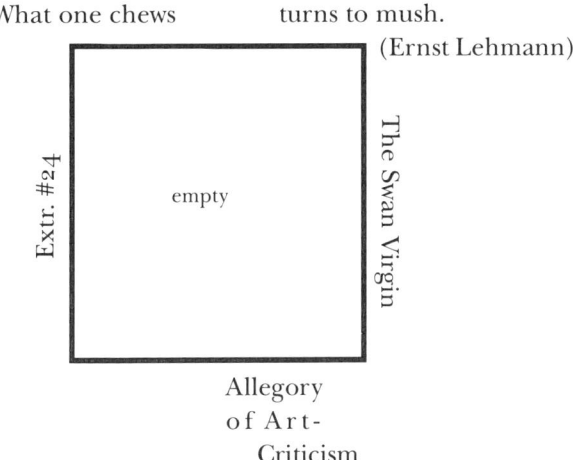

The author has created a strange allegory for good old Aartccriticism. It is a natural and faithful reproduction of the critiques in daily papers. The daily press on art, the so-called dailyartpress, wears a little girl's dress. Chaste and modest, it has tied a tiny apron over it, with embroidery trimmings, not to be confused with embroilery rimmings. Legs she's got none, just about sold out. So what could she use to walk on? Her hands. But those are so to say inclusive of arms also just about sold out. So what could she use to grab on to? The head. But the head is nothing more than a clothes hanger. On it hangs the dailyartpress with embroidery trimmings. So what could she use to think? For this purpose the author has supplied her with a reserve-head, as one already finds them near the torsos of old Egyptian kings in their tombchambers in the pyramids.[1] The head has the characteristic, odd, barking expression of the art critics, glasses on the nose and a headscarf covering the missing mind. The nose is red. He who has worries, needs liquor.

So how come this could be an introduction? Sir, it is first of all a question of bribing the critics, so that they'll fill out good report cards for my book. He who oils well, travels well.

Kurt Schwitters

[1] See Peliareus Museum, Hildesheim.

AUGUSTA BOLTE[2] saw about 10 people on the street, who all advanced in one and the same direction. This seemed suspicious to Augusta Bolte, very suspicious indeed. 10 people were walking in one and the same direction. 1, 2, 3, 4, 5, 6, 7, 8, 9, 10. Something was going on there. For otherwise 1, 2, 3, 4, 5, 6, 7, 8, 9, 10 people would not be walking in one and the same direction. Because when nothing's going on, then 1, 2, 3, 4, 5, 6, 7, 8, 9, 10 people would not walk in the exact same direction, for then 1, 2, 3, 4, 5, 6, 7, 8, 9, 10 people would walk in 1, 2, 3, 4, 5, 6, 7, 8, 9, 10 different directions. That's for sure, and Miss Augusta Bolte had always been a brilliant girl, even back in school. But when something is going on, then 1, 2, 3, 4, 5, 6, 7, 8, 9, 10 people as a rule go in one and the same direction, and not in 1, 2, 3, 4, 5, 6, 7, 8, 9, 10 different directions. When something is going on, then 10, 20, 30, 40, 50, 60, 70, 80, 90, 100 people can also go in one and the same direction. When something is going on even 100, 200, 300, 400, 500, 600, 700, 800, 900, 1000 people can go in one and the same direction. That, and much else, Augusta knew. For example, Augusta musta known that she had to rhyme with musta. Augusta counted. There really were 1, 2, 3, 4, 5, 6, 7, 8, 9, 10 people exactly who were going in one and the same direction. Why exactly? Who could have had the effrontery to exactly count these 1, 2, 3, 4, 5, 6, 7, 8, 9, 10 people? But somebody musta done it because the borderline is 9. Because when 9 people, i.e., when exactly 1, 2, 3, 4, 5, 6, 7, 8, 9 people go in one and the same direction, something may be going on, though it is not absolutely necessary that something should be going on. The number 10, however, is restlessly convincing, i.e., when exactly 1, 2, 3, 4, 5, 6, 7, 8, 9, 10 are going in exactly one and the same direction, then in a way something must exactly be going on. But what? Here it was clear for Augusta, and here clear and here rhyme, that something musta been going on, and here Augusta and musta rhymed again. But, as already said, what? It was clear to her that she would never never find out, if she asked one of the 1, 2, 3, 4, 5, 6, 7, 8, 9, 10 people, because each individual, i.e., 1, 2, 3, 4, 5, 6, 7, 8, 9, 10 is so mean, where mean

[2]Augusta Bolte, Anna Blume, and Arnold Böcklin all start with the same letters: A.B.

is the only fitting expression for such a meanness, that he keeps his, in a way, each one's his, news exclusively for himself. Augusta knew this, in school she had already been a gifted student, in a way. And now? How now? A scandalous rhyme! How rhymed with now. Beyond that it seemed especially peculiar to Miss Augusta that not only did how rhyme with now, but now also rhymed with how. And meanwhile the 1, 2, 3, 4, 5, 6, 7, 8, 9, 10 people went their way in a way. Augusta however remained as if suspended in thought for a short span of time, in a way as if rooted to her spot, like a tree in a way, as she discovered the unheard of rhyme between how and now on the one and on the other hand. The rhyme repeated on her. Like liveroil. Augusta swallowed. For when something's happening then the most unrhymed things happen to happen. Then all of a sudden what never rhymed before, rhymes. Let's sum up! 1, 2, 3, 4, 5, 6, 7, 8, 9, 10 people were walking in one and the same direction, now rhymed with how. Something obviously had to be going on. How should Augusta find out? Never, if she asked one of the 1, 2, 3, 4, 5, 6, 7, 8, 9, 10 people for each single person kept its wisdom for itself. Just so as to anger Augusta. It was a scandalous insolence that there was not a single decent human being with a noble soul among them who would come and tell Augusta all. Augusta was simply not considered to be all there. No civilized person should permit something like that to happen. How now? A really eerie rhyme. Something had to be done, otherwise the most scandalous things could happen to Augusta. Like possibly being choked to death by rhymes. Alliteration would be added and if by chance she were stuck into a metric pattern, that would be it. Then she would probably be treated like an old spinster, she who had been such a brilliant girl, so gifted even back in school, and no one would tell anything that was interesting anymore. This must not happen to a woman like Augusta. Something had to happen here. 1, 2, 3, 4, 5, 6, 7, 8, 9, 10 people were going accurately in one and the same direction, now rhyming oddly with how, nobody told Augusta what was happening. This went against her grain. For a moment she wondered what that grain was, against which, in a way, it went. Then she hitched up her skirt and all her manliness and ran after the 10, 9, 8, 7, 6, 5, 4, 3, 2, 1 people.

But what was this? At the next street corner 5 split off from the other 5 and went down one street, while the remaining 5 went down the other street. Of course Augusta took this to be an infamous ruse, a brazen deception. The 10 people had in a way silently said to each other that Augusta would notice that they were going in one and the same direction. Augusta would draw her conclusions from this; for example, that something was going on. These 10 people reckoned in a way that Augusta would show the normal intelligence of the average person. They also had told themselves in silence, that Miss Augusta Bolte would try to find out what it was that was going on. Augusta would follow and follow them and in this simple way finally see what she wanted to hear, or, in other words, what was going on, in a way, what was in fact happening. Oh, Augusta knew mass psychosis when she saw it, even back in school she had been a very gifted girl. But an old spinster shouldn't know everything. And so in order to deceive Miss Augusta, they had split up in silence. Augusta could only follow 5 people, they knew that Augusta could not split herself up. For various reasons. I.e., the reasons here didn't matter, but it had been a scandalous impertinence of the mass to split up or, better, to divide.

Augusta however was a decisive person and quickly decided to follow one of the 5. Augusta however was also conscientious, had, in a way, character. Well, could it have been the other 5? Salty doubts were simmering in her poor, tortured skull, somewhat like sauerkraut. It seemed so suspicious to her that it should be 5.[3] She took a few more steps and then the inspiration came to her that it musta been the other 5. But what musta been? At any rate she thought better of it and followed the other 5. For Miss Augusta could not see why she shouldn't follow these 5 rather than the other 5. 5 equals 5, and 5 people equal 5 people, except for individual characteristics, which however in this special case didn't count in a way. Thus she followed the other 5. But for all that, and that was exactly the shrewd aspect of it, for the same reason why she followed the other 5, she could also have followed the one 5, the first 5. Why indeed did 10 people have to split up into groups of 5. That kind of thing was a shrewd tactic of

[3] And 5 happens to be an uneven number.

the, in a way, hostile mass. For indeed in this case it absolutely did not matter which of the two groups of 5 people Augusta should follow. The salty doubts began to boil over. But Augusta had always been a brilliant girl, even back in school. Though she was no crammer. And thus she hit upon the only correct solution. Given that she had the choice between 2 identical groups of 5 in terms of quantity, to be accurate she had to follow each 5 in equal proportion, especially in relation to the duration of the walk. To put it vulgarly, she first had to follow the one 5 for a certain time, then the other 5 for the same length of time, then the first 5, then the other 5, the first 5, etcetera, etcetera. Thus: Augusta lost no time thinking, but quickly made up her mind and turned and ran back to the street corner, let's see what the one 5 is up to. As it so happened that both groups of 5 were walking on steadily, the distance between them and the street corner kept growing and growing, and so Augusta musta run, again this eerie rhyme, because the distance simply kept growing. Well now, Augusta was young, and anyway she did it in a way for health reasons. Now, Augusta as said was a brilliant female. Always already had been. And she knew what to do when she had to run faster and faster. To begin with she first jettisoned all unnecessary ballast. Like a ship that drops everything nonessential when it wants to sink, so that at least not everything sinks at the same time, so did she jettison, as it was in a way now also a matter of life and death, her hat with hatneedle, her gloves, her pocketbook with handkerchief and purse, her pince-nez, rings, and bracelets, as in this case completely unnecessary ballast, and ran now after this 5 now after the other 5 by shuttling around the corner. All the while Augusta admired her presence of mind, the fact that despite her hurry she still knew what to do, that she had to jettison ballast. Again a case of rhyming, as knew rhymed with do and do with knew. Again it rhymed in an unbelievably ridiculous and obvious way, in a way. It all suggested something extraordinary. And Augusta shuttled as said, meanwhile and during, between and around the corner and doing this she felt the inner satisfaction that, no matter how hard it was, she was fulfilling her duty fully and completely, and indeed the faster she had to run the more deeply she felt this. Except that she was getting hot, and her clothes were swinging around her knees. But Augusta had always been a quick thinking and decisive girl. Now while running she pondered that she would have to increase her speed, if in future she wanted to remain in contact with both the one 5 and the other 5, whose distance between themselves and the streetcorner was increasing regularly, and the idea, self-evident and, in a way as plain as the nose on her face, came to her that she also had to consider her skirt and blouse as unnecessary ballast. At the same time she was pleased that despite her high speed she still managed such a nice play on words, and in a way she firmly focused her eye on the idea that was as plain as the nose on her face and got rid of further ballast. Then she started running in the direction of the one 5 and the other 5. But no one can escape their fate. The distance between the two groups of 5 had eventually become so great that Augusta, even using her utmost speed, could count on only one more successful attempt in rejoining the 5 after turning the streetcorner. There always comes a point when a human being has to make a final decision. That's man's inhuman fate. No matter how sad it is in and of itself. And thus did Augusta overcome her salty misgivings viz., should she follow the one 5 or the other 5, and decided to run around the corner one more time in order to catch the one 5.

Barely had a slightly heated up Augusta Bolte reached the one 5, when suddenly a young girl separated from them and without a word or a good-bye, in a way as if it was the most natural thing to do, went into a house. What now? The rhyme is how. Which didn't help Augusta one little bit. The only right thing would have been to return now to the other 5. But fate had in a way borne witness[4] against Augusta. Because she could no longer get back to the other 5, the distance had become too great. On the other hand the choice was now much easier. Between 1, 4, and 5 people it was self-evident that the 5 had to be chosen. For Augusta that was, the rhyme here is, clear. But Augusta was a brilliantined girl, even backmost in school, as well as decisive. She could no longer catch up with the 5, so the choice remained between the 4 and the one. Making a quick decision, which just happened to be the way Augusta Bolte happened to be, even

[4] Concerning witness, cf. "tribunal."

back in school she had been a brilliantined girl, she followed the 4, but not before having made a note, from sheer conscientiousness, of the number of the house into which the one had disappeared. That had been the number 5. Of all numbers it had to be 5. Now what, for example, was the meaning of that? One split from 5 and went into 5. That was unusual. It had to mean something. All of this, and among other things also the many rhymes, strengthened Augusta's accurate perception that something had to be going on here which she absolutely wanted to find out about. For otherwise why would her name be Bolte? There's a reason to rhyme all one's life with bold. Having thought this, Augusta decisively followed, as said, the four. A young person needs luck. To begin with Augusta now wiped away the beads of sweat, cooled down a bit, and rejoiced in her heart that she could now relax somewhat as the 4 sauntered along very gemütlich, in a way as if nothing had happened. All the while Augusta musta known, again that eerie rhyme, that something anyway was going on. If not why would the 4 keep walking in one and the same direction?

All of a sudden they reached a crossing. And as if the devil had a hand in it, 2 took a right and 2 took a left. How now?

Again this eerie, this tormenting rhyme. Augusta musta known, which already again rhymed tormentingly, that she didn't know what she should do. How now. That was more than a human being could endure, triple rhyme in less than 30 seconds. Augusta musta known, the fourth rhyme, that the whole matter had in a way now entered a critical stage. Augusta was firmly decided to enter after it, in a way. For Augusta already knew the system from her experience in following the two groups of 5 people. Augusta was in a way able to write a tactical manual for the pursuit of 2 identical groups of people, she was so well oriented. And she was willing to reapply this, her tactic in the pursuit of 2 groups of people of 2 persons each. History would some day call this the Miss-Augusta-Tactic, and with one fell swoop she'd be ripe for history. So, Miss Augusta now started to follow the one group of two for a specific time span. Then she turned around and followed the other group of 2 for the same time span. For how could she have known which of the 2 it was? How could anybody at all have known which were the correct 2? Or rather was. Not was. Were was the right conjunctive. Were was the right infinitive. All the while Augusta still thought that it was rather eerie that in such rather difficult situations certain foreign words were still present. Who for example would now want to know something about foreign words, which otherwise furnish life so pleasantly? And Augusta turned around again, away from the direction of the one two and into the direction of the other two. How pleasant that this time she didn't need to shuttle around the corner any more, for the 2 2-ers walked in exactly opposite directions. How pleasant that every evil still contains its share of good. Someone's barely dead and instantly he can afford a coffin, even if during his lifetime he couldn't have afforded a single nail. That's the kind of thing Augusta called luck. And meanwhile the distance between each group of 2 grew larger and larger. Augusta ran hither and thither, hither and thither, until finally she was confronted once again with the decision to make a decision as to which of the 2 she should end up following. But anyhow in a way she already knew the system. For the system was based on the Miss-Augusta-Tactic. A special case didn't ask for a big decision. What always matters is the system. And in the life of a human being there often comes a point where the either-or ceases, a point of no return in a way, something like a wall on which it is written: "Up to here and no further!" Augusta knew this way of reasoning through her tactic. Augusta was a brilliant girl, had always been, even backmost in school. Without being a crammer. But it was especially in the school of life that Augusta was brilliantined. Life was a hard school. Only brilliantined people can live life. Life is a high education. In a way, a higher education. And in that institution of higher education Miss Augusta Bolte wanted to get her doctorate, become a Doctor of Life, so to speak, a Dr. Lif. And this was going to be her doctoral dissertation. The subject was crying out for treatment, for up until now it had been treated very little, a thankful subject. What position would Augusta then be in, if she were Dr. of Life, Miss Dr. Augusta, Miss Dr. Lif. A new faculty. This and several other things, for example the word "infinitive," Augusta, whose name means the "sublime" in German, was pondering while she definitively separated herself from the other 2, so as from now on to run after only the one 2. Augusta now estimated her speed to be the speed of sound, 333 and 1/3 meters per sec. A further acceleration seemed impossible to her, for otherwise she would arrive before one could hear her footsteps, and the thunder of her steps would follow on her heels. Now, Augusta was just as modest as she was bright, and so she modestly asserted that she would no longer leave the one 2, and that she would follow them until she found out what was going on.

   Suddenly those last two also split up, one entering a house on the right, the other entering a house on the left. Miss Dr. Augusta (I will already call you that here honoris causa),[5] stood in the street like a man. On the left one hope disappeared into a house and on the right one hope disappeared into a house. On the right one hope disappeared into a house and on the left one hope disappeared into a house. Miss Dr. Augusta was a brilliantined girl. She thought of the word "infinitive." All of a sudden the word "tree" shot through her head in a way. That is to say, it did not shoot at all in fact. For as Miss Dr. Augusta kept feeling her head, it had remained whole all around. For if the word had or had been shot, there would have had to be a hole in her head. That is to say, and to be exact, 2 holes, for a word couldn't just shoot into her head, it had to, because of the great speed, shoot through her head. Life a rifle bullet. Suddenly Miss Augusta took fright, for she found both her earholes. 2 holes, the one on the left, the other on the right. That had to attract attention. Could it be that the word had shot through both earholes and opened these two openings? But then it would have bled. But it did not bleed. And amidst all this Miss Dr. Augusta had meanwhile forgotten which word it was that had shot. She could not remember. Moreover and as already stated nothing seemed to have, or to have been, shot. Words don't shoot that easily. Still, it made her uneasy that maybe eventually a word could have shot, though it may have been a cold shot. This, just like the extraordinarily copious rhymes in everyday language that Miss Dr. Augusta used with herself, confirmed her in the indubitably correct feeling that something had to be happening. And besides, someone had

[5] For honor's sake.

disappeared in a house on the right and someone on the left. Miss Dr. Augusta admired her own calm concerning these matters. Something was happening, and she didn't know it, she still didn't know it. And now she started to ponder what was to be done here. The old rhyme of how and now had guided her so well so far. It guided Augusta until she musta known. The rhyme surrounded her like old poetry. Which one of the two she now should follow was difficult to decide upon. One equals one, at least in terms of quantity. In itself it was indeed relatively indifferent which one of the two Miss Dr. Augusta should now follow. In her mind, for Miss Dr. Augusta had indeed a mind, she saw herself already shuttling for hours back and forth between the two opposite houses. For she knew the tactic, for the system had not changed. Augusta knew that the distance between the two opposite standing houses would steadily grow larger and larger, until finally it finally grew so large that Augusta would again have to decide which one of the two she would definitively have to follow, because despite all her efforts, given the great distances, she would not be able to keep up the shuttling back and forth between the two houses. But when at the end she would finally have made a decision, then that one would suddenly split up in two halves. And the one half would disappear into one room, and the other half into the other. Which half should Augusta then follow? In and of itself it would again be indifferent. Miss Dr. Lif would thus shuttle once again between two rooms lying next to and opposite each other while constantly moving away from each other. Finally the distance between the rooms would be so great that Miss Dr. Augusta would have to make a decision yet again. The half would then divide into two quarters, the one quarter would sit down on one chair, the other on another. The distance between the two chairs would grow constantly, Miss Dr. would shuttle, finally decide for one quarter, which would then divide into 2 eighths, the one eighth would sit down on one half of a chair, the other on the other. Miss Dr. A. Bolte knew the system, and with it and through it, science. But she also had learned something through the precedents.[6] Her tactic in regard to the system had simply been wrong. On the other hand

---

[6] A rare animal, lives in Siberia, has highly valued fur.

she didn't know another tactic right away. She would finally experience the progressive division of the eighth into a sixteenth, a thirtysecond, sixtyfourth, onehundredtwentyeighth, all the way down to the atom, and she was afraid that, as far as her doctoral dissertation was concerned, nothing would remain about which she could ask what was happening. So many thoughts were now shooting through Miss Dr. Augusta's head, that the latter had turned into a sieve and seemed to possess several thousand ears. At least it seemed that way to Miss Dr. Experience is the greatest science. The tactic was wrong. In the end Miss Dr. Augusta would have wasted her strength, and the 10 people would have dissolved into roughly a billion parts. Yes, even back in school Augusta had been a brilliant girl. At any rate, our degenerate culture needs consistent people. Miss Dr. Augusta Bolte was consistent; there is no question that she had character.

Miss Dr. Augusta decisively—which is how she was—decided henceforth to go look for the one young lady who had disappeared into the one house by splitting off from the remaining four. Augusta did find the street again and entered the house. The first floor door said: "Mrs. driedplumproducerswidow Alma Schulz." The title seemed suspicious to Augusta. She rang the bell and when a woman opened the door, she said: "Did a young girl, who had just split off from her five companions on the street, come in here about one hour ago?" Mrs. driedplumproducerswidow thought that maybe it had been in the apartment opposite. Miss Dr. Augusta now rang the bell on the opposite door and asked: "Did a young girl, who had just split off from her five companions, come in here about one hour ago?" The lady in question said: "Maybe the other flat?" So Miss Dr. Augusta rang the truly secret plumproducerswidow Alma Schulz's bell again and told the lady when she opened the door, that the lady from vis-à-vis[7] had sent her back over here and so she was using the occasion once more to ask if maybe a young girl, having just split off from her five companions, had come in here about one hour ago. Mrs. driedplumproducerswidow Alma Schulz said, maybe it had been on the second floor. Now Miss Dr. Bolte rang the bell on the second floor and asked, if maybe a young girl had come in

[7] A French word.

there roughly an hour ago, having just previously split off from her 4 companions. The lady in question said: "Maybe first floor." And so Miss Dr. Augusta rang the first floor bell again and asked Mrs. true driedplumproducerswidow, if maybe a young girl had come in there roughly an hour ago, who would have just previously split off from her 4 companions. Mrs. true driedplumproducercouncilor denied it politely yet firmly and said: "Maybe you should check the third floor, for here she ain't."[8] Miss Dr. A. Bolte now also asked on the third, fourth, fifth, and sixth floors in both the left and the right apartments. Inbetween she was sent repeatedly to Mrs. true driedplumproducercouncilor, who, after repeated and polite but firm denegations, finally started to hem and haw hoarsely. This did not help her highdried councilor. For Miss Dr. Augusta returned one more time, rang the bell and asked, if maybe a young girl had come in roughly an hour or so ago—"2 and 1/2 hours," Mrs. councilor corrected—right, if a young girl had in a way come in 2 and 1/2 hours ago—"who would have just previously split off from her 4 companions," Mrs. true dried councilor completed the sentence. And all at once Mrs. plumcouncilor, while taking the whole affair for a plum, became more unpleasant than Miss Dr. Augusta had either expected or earned. After repeated hemming and hawing, she[9] smirked, wagged both hands[10] as if she was trying to weigh the air, hit the door repeatedly with the flat of her hand, and thus accidentally broke the pane. Then she screamed: "Pee, pee, pee, pee, pee" but her voice cramped and she ran out of the house and called the fire department. Break glass, push button, wait for someone to come. She did not wait, however, but went back, grabbed her wire doormat and brought it down vertically with a force of approximately 2 horsepower over Miss Dr. Augusta's much-tried head. Miss Dr. Augusta noticed this right away, and in a disagreeable way; as she was beginning to feel uncomfortable she walked with dignity toward the back of the house so as to ask there in the same way after the young girl who had, roughly 3 hours ago, split off from her 4 comrades to enter house number 5. Immediately she noticed 3, 4, 5. That's rhythm. But she couldn't think back and forth on why this should be important

[8]Provincial expression.   [9]Mrs. councilor.   [10]Like a dog.

for long, because due to the quick climbing up and down she got a cramp in the calf of her leg. This was very unpleasant for her. She was in something of a hurry. Inquisitive faces stared from every door. And Miss Dr. Augusta had to remain calm, all the while her calf ached vividly. She started to reflect on the concepts of ram and cramp in the calf. Ram is in a way a cramp of the calf in the foot, and a cramp in the calf is in a way a ram in the lower thigh. Lockjaw is somewhat similar. And in a way it was lucky that Miss Dr. Augusta did not have lockjaw instead of a cramp in the calf. She could also suddenly have caught softening of the brain, and then she would have had to give up the pursuit of her grandiose idea before its time. Augusta was a thankful creature, and she told all the people standing in their open doors how good it was that she only had a cramp in the calf. "Ya gotta whup it witha felt shoe," one lady suggested. Miss Dr. asked for a felt shoe and could now again take up the pursuit of her idea. On the sixth floor, second door, she was told that the lady had maybe gone into No. 5, as this was No. 6. Dr. Augusta said "thank you" and went to the next house, front court and back court, each with 12 apartments. Meanwhile the cramp came back, so she once again borrowed a felt shoe. Suddenly she lost a heel. But how much could that count, compared to eternity? And on the sixth floor, back court, second door, she was told she should try No. 5, as this was 5A. Miss Dr. Augusta was a brilliant girl, even back in school. She knew that practice makes perfect and that the longer she had to search for the young woman, the more certain she would be of finding her. That's what practice brings. Suddenly one finds what one thought one is still searching for. That's what practice brings. But this time Augusta wanted to make sure that she would not again mistake the house number. So she stopped a gentleman in the street and asked him to point out No. 5 to her. Miss Augusta musta known, again this eerie rhyme, that she, by being Miss Dr., was a personality, and that everyone would willingly bend to her authority. Everyone had to tell her where and when No. 5 was. She was a personality, just like the very great personalities of great times. And it did not matter a bit that she was standing there in her slip,[11] for clothes don't

---

[11] Roughly like art criticism.

make the man, it is something that comes from the inside. A pity that she had lost her heel. The gentleman however was called Mayer. Mayer was a man of the world. Mayer bowed deeply and elegantly and called Miss Dr. Augusta "Dear Lady." Then he asked sympathetically if she had lost her pince-nez, while tactfully avoiding noticing her missing low heel. Mayer then showed her No. 5. Miss Dr. Augusta asked one more time if he was sure that that was No. 5. Yes, without a doubt it was No. 5. And, bowing formally, Mayer went on his way. But due to her previous experiences, Miss Dr. Augusta had become suspicious and therefore asked a second man about No. 5. That man was called Müller. Miss Dr. Augusta knew that because of her personality everybody had to answer her. Thus she asked Müller to tell her where No 5 was. Müller was by profession a toiletcleaner. Müller just mumbled between his missing teeth: "Is the bitch blind?" Augusta asked one more time: "Oh please, sir, be kind enough to show me the number 5 for I do suffer from leg cramps." "I'll show 'er," Müller mulled it over and showed her No. 4. Thus Augusta asked after the young lady in the 24 apartments of the number 4. Finally, she was sent to No. 3. But what a lucky break, what a sign from heaven! Augusta had always been a brilliantined girl,[12] and she had always had these premonitions. And thus it happened by chance that Miss Dr. Augusta, wanting to go to No. 3, wound up in No. 5. Movement makes for hunger, and hunger makes for satiation. Movement is the best cook. Meaning that food was not even to be given a thought. At any rate Augusta was now in No. 5, instinct had run away with her. And indeed, after she had asked in all 10 apartments of the front court and in all 10 apartments of the back court after the young girl, she recognized the young lady in question who roughly 6 hours ago had separated from the 5 in order to enter 5. The questioned lady in question herself opened the door of the sixth floor, rear, apartment.[13] Instinct had simply run away with Miss Dr. Lif., how else could she have found the young girl so quickly. How happy Augusta was that the young girl had not moved or died in the meantime. But what should Augusta say now? At any rate, this time she wanted to go about things adroitly. Augusta knew that

[12] *Vide* critics.   [13] Sixth floor, of all things.

she must proceed diplomatically. Otherwise she wouldn't learn anything. Augusta knew that she had to safeguard her personal authority. A genial thought came to her, like a beau, and shot through her shot through head. And like a ricochet, the thought remained stuck. Augusta felt that now she quasi-stood face to face with eternity and that's why she remained silent. Augusta remained silent. "What do you want?" asked the young girl. Miss Dr. Augusta safeguarded her personal authority and remained silent. "How can I be of service to you?" the girl asked further. Miss Dr. Augusta remained silent. "What do you want here?" — Augusta knew how to safeguard her personal authority. Now the young girl started to scream into her ear, what it was that she wanted. Miss Dr. Lif wasn't deaf at all in fact, only at times a personality, nothing more. But Miss Dr. Augusta was upset because of this behavior toward a personality, even though she felt some satisfaction at having made such a profound impression. For in relation to personalities, a well-behaved person tends to be calm, friendly and quiet. Though when personalities go deaf, then they can't hear anything anyway. One puts one's finger on one's mouth and one says respectfully: "There she stands, the personality. She does not make a sound. Do you hear how she remains silent?"

And all at once the girl slammed the door shut.

Miss Dr. Augusta started to ring the bell again. The young girl didn't answer. Miss Dr. rang the bell again. The young girl opened. Miss Dr. Augusta remained silent, she safeguarded her personality. So the girl slammed the door shut again.

Miss Dr. Augusta started to ring the bell for the third time. The young girl didn't come. Miss Dr. started to ring more loudly. A dog started to bark. Many dogs came and barked. The young girl didn't come. Miss Dr. Augusta rang the bell very loudly and banged with her hand against the panes. Now the dogs were barking very loudly. People emerged from all the doors. Then the young girl came out again. Miss Dr. remained silent. The girl was upset, she trembled and said: "Would you please tell me finally what it is that you want." — Miss Dr. Augusta gazed at her with contempt. One must tame the beasts. "I demand," screamed the young girl, "that you tell me what it is that you want, or else that you leave the house." "That's outrageous," a voice called from below. Miss Dr. Augusta remained silent. But the dogs barked more loudly. Now the young girl had to weep.

That's when Miss Dr. Augusta felt satisfaction that her tactical silence tactic had been the right one. Besides that she was busy fighting a new leg cramp. She now abandoned her tactic, walked up to the young girl, took the latter's head between her hands and laid it gently on her breast. The young girl wept up and down. Just as the leg cramp started anew, the youngish girl wept over. The dogs had grown hoarse. One of them wanted to bite into Miss Dr. Augusta's ill leg. That was a major piece of luck, for otherwise the two women would still be standing on the staircase.

Suddenly Miss Dr. Augusta entered the apartment as if it belonged to her, and in a friendly voice asked the young girl to follow her and to take a seat. Miss Dr. Augusta was an authority. That's why the young girl followed her. "Sit down," the person of authority now told the youngish girl. "What's your name?" — "Anna." — "And your last name?" — "Sündig?" — "And what other first names did your dear parents give you?" — "Louise, Eilerdine." — "But Anna is the name you answer to." — "Yes." — "How old are you, Anna Sündig?" — "Thirtyseven." — "That young!" — "Indeed." — "Draft status?" — "Draftable."[14] — "Military size?" — "6 foot 2." — "Weight?" — "Slender." — "Any illnesses?" — "Heart." — "Military rank?" — "Crooked, not straight." — "Civilian profession?" — "Bunion masseuse." — "Single?" — "In a way." — "Do you know how to cook?" — "For home use only." — "In that case, brew us a strong cup of tea." — The young girl put water on gas. Meanwhile, with the young girl gone, Miss Augusta reflected.

"Reflection is no light," my grandmother used to say. Miss Dr. Augusta however reflected to herself that she was not going to find out anything this way. I.e., she found out all kinds of things, but not what she wanted to know. Odd occurrences had occurred, and Miss Dr. Augusta knew that, but not what. A new inaudible rhyme. Strange that -at and -at should not rhyme. Augusta now asked in a different way in order to find out what

[14]Older reading: laughable.

was going on. First Miss Dr. Bolte asked if the young girl was the lady who, having separated from the 5, had entered the No 5. The young girl denied it. And yet it certainly had been her. Augusta knew it for sure. Otherwise Augusta wouldn't have asked. One doesn't ask when one doesn't know the answer. It had certainly been her, certainly. Bolte now told her to her face that it had been her. Like a wire doormat brought down with approximately 2 horsepower, so did Miss Dr. Bolte now bring down on her head the fact that she had first been one of a group of 10 persons who had walked in one and the same direction, that she and 4 others had then separated from the group, and that she had finally left the four to go into 5. Annalouise Sündig disputed these facts. And Augusta had gone to the trouble of finding this ungrateful creature. Augusta had put up with every acceleration, had jettisoned all unnecessary ballast, had felt a doormat on her head and cramps in her calves, and this creature who knew everything wouldn't even own up to what Augusta herself already knew. She lied. The creature lied. Now Augusta asked: "Haven't I jettisoned enough ballast for you? Should I now also put the cotton in my ears on the table?" And she put two small cotton wads on the table.

"You can't really expect that for your sake I should also take off my slip. You brazen creature, you blockhead! And because of you her Excellency, Mrs. truly secret driedplumproducercouncilor Alma Schultz brought down her highborn wire doormat on my head with approximately 2 horsepower. And now you idiot you lie to me! Did I get my two leg cramps for nothing?" And with that Augusta became very angry. And while pointing with her finger to the table and saying, "There, there is the cotton," she tore a leg off the writing desk. Annalouise Sündig grabbed both her legs and held them tightly. With the aforementioned leg of the writing desk, Augusta Bolte destroyed the windows so that the panes fell down into the street, then the table, the chairs, a small dresser, pictures, mirror, knickknacks, etcetera. The pictures on the wall stepped out of their frames and Miss Annalouise took flight. Meanwhile the tea was burning. This may possibly be the only occasion in the history of the world in which tea burned. A large cloud blew through the small apartment, somewhat like worms. Augusta Bolte pondered how easily she could have become sheepishly overwrought if, instead of cramps, she had gotten rams. The occupants of the house, scared by the noise of the breaking panes, began to gather. There was nothing more she could find out here, that much Augusta knew. And with the dignity of an authority she left the building,[15] while telling the inhabitants she met to run upstairs because the tea was burning and there was danger that it might explode.

When they all started to run upstairs, Miss Dr. Augusta Bolte stepped out into the street and sent all the people she met into No. 5 because something had happened there. One man called Augusta a harmless madwoman, a remark that inflamed her hot anger even more. But then she tore herself loose from the burning tea and once again stood with both legs firmly anchored in reality. For the situation demanded Augusta's undivided attention. Augusta knew that something unheard of had happened, and that something was something Augusta Bolte wanted to know. 1, 2, 3, 4, 5, 6, 7, 8, 9, 10 people had walked in one and the same direction. Enough reason for something to have happened. But here nothing more could be learned. Thus Augusta knew that Augusta had to learn about it in some other way. Something in a way was still in the air. Just why did everybody look at her, Augusta Bolte, that way? Nobody does such a thing without good reason. Therefore something had to be going on. There was nothing special about her. Probably every woman wore a slip and a shirt, so that was nothing special. Augusta was a brilliant girl, had always been, even back in school. But this was a very difficult doctoral dissertation. The doctorate in Lif studies is among the most difficult.

To begin with Miss Dr. Augusta decided to wait once more until 1, 2, 3, 4, 5, 6, 7, 8, 9, 10 people would be walking in one and the same direction. But reasoning by coincidence with other great events (again an eerie rhyme, -dence and -vents), Augusta musta known (here gusta and musta rhymed) that truly great events always announce themselves in different ways. She was truly brilliantined. So, Augusta musta known, and did, that if 1,

[15] Compare art crticism.

2, 3, 4, 5, 6, 7, 8, 9, 10 people were now indeed seen walking in one and the same direction, it would not mean anything this time, not even that something was happening. Augusta did not want to be had.[16]

While she was still pondering this, 1, 2, 3, 4, 5, 6, 7, 8, 9, 10 little girls walked in one and the same direction, and the girls' boarding school met Miss Dr. Augusta. Augusta counted: "1, 2, 3, 4, 5, 6, 7, 8, 9, 10." Okay, but for what reason should great events always announce themselves in different ways? For what reason? Augusta found no reason. In and of themselves they could announce themselves either differently or in the same way. Thus Augusta, as a conscientious human being, had to follow the 10 girls just as at the beginning she had followed those 10 people. And that's what Augusta did. But while she was following the boarding school, the thought came to her that, because great events were able to announce themselves differently, she could also discover the truth in a different way, i.e., if, rather than following the 10 girls, she were to walk in the opposite direction. And so Augusta started by walking in the opposite direction. But as Augusta simply did not know if it was more correct to follow the 10 girls or to walk in the opposite direction, and as, in a way, it did not matter in the face of eternity, she started to shuttle back and forth once again. Augusta was a logical human being, even if it wasn't always easy. At this point Miss Augusta thought of the great inventors throughout history. Wasn't the situation rather similar? In a way at least. For what, in truth, is certain on this earth? Thus, for example, if someone wanted to invent gunpowder, how should he go about it? Even if for example he pulverized everything, that still wouldn't ensure that he'd get gunpowder.[17] Maybe he would even have to leave many things unground, for nothing can be recognized otherwise than through its contrary. Therefore, he who wanted to invent powder had to build blocks. But what kind of powder anyway? There was for example gunpowder, chest powder, baking powder, cleansing powder, healing powder, depending on what the inventor in question had ground up. And things were in fact even more complicated. Thus chest powder, for example, does

[16]Compare epigonic running after.   [17]Once more compare art criticism.

not necessarily need to be pulverized chest. On the other hand it could indeed be pulverized chest. For who could keep you from calling pulverized chest something else besides chest powder? And how would one pulverize chest anyway? One would at least have to start by drying it very thoroughly. And then there is a vast choice of breasts and chests. There is, for example, goose breast, chest of drawers, breastbone, breast stroke, goose liver, goose liver paté, salami, knackwurst, doll kitchens, etcetera. This Miss Dr. Augusta pondered as she repeatedly changed direction, either running after the boarding school or in the opposite direction. In the process, the distance between the boarding school and the place where Augusta had discovered the same, kept growing, and Augusta's speed meanwhile had reached 333 and 1/3. She thought again about new, unheard of things that would happen as harbingers of great events. Then she saw a man in the distance who, when he caught sight of her, turned around horrified and took flight. Now Miss Dr. Lif set herself in motion at much higher speed, in the direction of the fleeing man. The latter ran away as if whipped by furies. In order to catch up with the fugitive, Augusta now jettisoned further ballast, i.e., her slip. The speed reached by her has been estimated at 5–6 hundred meters per sec. Suddenly the man jumped into a hackney cab and disappeared.

Miss Dr. Augusta now stood there like a decorative figure in a public space.[18] Given the distance, it had become impossible to catch up with the boarding school. The man had driven away in a hackney cab. But she didn't stand there long. Suddenly she jumped into a car, and the car pursued the hackney cab like in the movies.

But now, as the car reached the hackney cab after a highspeed chase, Miss Dr. Lif Augusta Bolte began to reflect. For work is easy and full of joy when backed by gentle words. She was thinking that maybe it would be too one-sided to only pursue the man in the hackney cab; who could tell if this man was in fact the harbinger of great events? Couldn't it also be that the boarding school was a sign of major events to come? She could still reach it by car, viz. the boarding school. And so she gave the driver the

[18] Like a critic at an art exhibition.

necessary instructions and, according to her well-known system, she now set up a carshuttlemovement between manhackneycab and tengirlboardingschool. Until another thought hit her.

To begin with one would have to say something about Richard Eckemecker. His story is short. Who he was doesn't matter. For he was nothing else than Richard Eckemecker, descended from old Eckemecker, didn't disresemble his father and his dear mother, and had inherited from his father a certain shyness, especially in relation to human beings. (Nonsense Augusta—it's marry you musta.) It was old Eckemecker who had coined the famous saying: "Man is an ass, yes, even an asshole." (Nonsense Augusta—it's marry you musta.) Little Richard had already been shy as a little child. He hated animals. Flies smarted, bees stung, ants nipped, snakes bit, horses and asses kicked, lions bit, cats scratched, etcetera. (Nonsense Augusta—it's marry you musta.) An asshole, it seemed to him, smarted, stung, nipped, bit, kicked, bit, scratched, and even shot, as much as it wanted. No wonder that little Richard became shy. (Nonsense Augusta—it's marry you musta.) He was shy in front of people. Like a horse. He did not mind single human beings, for no asshole has ever had courage. (According to Eckemecker, of course.) A lone asshole would never attack. But when in the majority, then the asshole became brave. (Nonsense Augusta—it's marry you musta.) And thus as soon as little Richard saw 2 or more humans, he became shy. His dear mother had therefore made up two neat little blinkers, so that he wouldn't have to see so many people all at once. Richard's condition had indeed somewhat improved, for 2 people no longer made him shy, though 3 did, at least when no other reasons forced him to suspect that he had been delivered into the hands of an asshole gone wild.

School had been out of the question. Richard had not shied from the teacher but from the other pupils, and had bolted every time, like a horse. Neither the carrot nor the stick had had any effect. And thus he hadn't been confirmed either. When in due time an attempt was made to turn him into a soldier, Richard demolished the barracks, was arrested and confronted by his sergeant; said noncom officer called him a.w.o.l. Richard understood asshole and had bailed out again. Like a bucket. And they let him run. Again like a bucket.

Now, on the very day that Augusta Bolte passed her Dr. Lif, Richard Eckemecker had gone for a walk on the street, wearing his blinkers as usual on the side of his head, not thinking about much. Then all of a sudden he met 1, 2, 3, 4, 5, 6, 7, 8, 9, 10 people, who came toward him from one and the same direction. Shy Richard had hardly caught sight of them when he became shy and bolted screaming, straight through the middle of the 1–10 people, who exploded all over the place. A young girl had not been able to save herself in time. Eckemecker had laid her out cold. (Nonsense Augusta—it's marry you musta.) Now the remaining nine had stopped and when they saw him running away, the asshole in them had woken up. The 9 people had pursued him, to do him harm. Now other people joined them, passers-by and one policeman. A wild chase began, with Eckemecker as its goal. Like in a movie. Richard didn't know what to do. So he ran through a plate glass window into a delicatessen shop. There he first toppled the owner then everything else. He toppled the fishtank, he toppled the jam shelves, he toppled the white cheese and the till, he toppled the sausage cupboard and the mustard pot, he toppled the sugarbag and the soft soap. The owner, Mr. Mayer, lay at the bottom. Now the pack of assholes drew close. While some of them began to loot, and the fish to jump, while others kept on demolishing, while others beat up the owner, a certain Mr. Mayer, while the police man, highly alarmed, squeezed off some warning shots, Richard Eckemecker escaped unnoticed through the private office and a corridor leading to another street.

There Richard Eckemecker now stood, sweating, foaming, and trembling like a horse. As if a noble horse had bolted. He removed his blinkers, to wipe off his forehead. Suddenly he perceived[19] a terrifying apparition. A woman in shirtsleeves, without corset, but with a slip and no dress, with totally twisted stockings, with one high and one low heel, her loosened hair fluttering in the wind, shaking her hands as if ready for action, such a woman was approaching him with dignity, like a person of

[19] German art critic term.

authority, running straight toward him. Shy Richard began to sob. Then all of a sudden he took off, like a man whipped by the already mentioned furies, took off, but this time not in the direction of the woman, but in the opposite direction. Terror burrowed eyelights in bowels. Richard Eckemecker felt an unspeakable horror. He jumped into a hackney cab and bolted. And as he shyly peeked back over his shoulder, he saw the woman jumping into a car. (Nonsense, Augusta—marry you musta.) What's going on, what does marrying mean here?

A terrortwisted chase ensued, like in a movie. Inbetween the car would race away, in order to catch up with the boarding school. Then it would return with fresh rage, like a village dog.[20] Suddenly it would dash away again, back to the tengirlboardingschool. The chase was terrortwisted, like in a movie.

Suddenly something shot through Miss Dr. Augusta's head again. A thought shot through it. Augusta remembered that in a way it did not matter in the face of eternity if she followed the man or not, just as it did not matter before if she followed the tengirlboardingschool or went in the opposite direction. Miss Dr. Lif had been a brilliant girl even back in school.[21] For who could know if the fleeing man was coming from great events or was in the process of running toward great events. Who would dare to decide if Miss Dr. Augusta must follow the man or drive in the opposite direction? And what was the opposite direction, anyway? Strictly speaking she would have had to walk in that opposite direction, and not drive, since the man for his part had come on foot from there. Salty doubts somersaulted. For who could know if, exactly because of the oppositeness, she wouldn't have had to drive in the opposite direction while running in the same direction? Who could know anything anyway? And it became clear to her that Dr. Lif couldn't know anything.[22] And in a hurry she felt the satisfaction of even now being, in a way, Miss Dr. Professor, or at least associate Professor, and this exactly because she couldn't know anything.

Suddenly the hackney cab stopped.

The man absconded into a house.

[20] Read art criticism.   [21] See above.
[22] The author appoints the critic as a Dr. Lif.

The die was cast, and the man had absconded into a house. Miss Professor Augusta had her car stop. It was clear that something was going on here. Why else should a man abscond into a house? You can't fit that into a hollow tooth! Why else should a man jump into a hackney cab to abscond into a house? Why? Something was certain: if nothing was happening here, then nothing was happening anywhere. Although the reverse could be true too. And while Augusta realized the equivalence of all values, as she now realized that, depending on one's taste, everything could prove everything or nothing, a new unheard of realization came to her, namely that it did not matter if one attended to it or not.

Nobody could attend to everything. Man had to make a choice. And he had to make a choice. And he had to make a choice, not because he had to make a choice, but because in itself it didn't matter if he made a choice or if he didn't make a choice.

In the face of this new realization, Miss Dr. Professor Augusta now drew a line through all of her previous life and decided that from now on she would dedicate her research powers wholly to the man who had absconded into the house. Everything was to be decided here. A pity that she couldn't drive the car into the house. Maybe this man would even marry her, when he learned that she was a Dr. Prof. Lif. Anyhow, should she marry sometime, this would be the right man for her. Because this man showed respect for her. This man considered her—since it was her due given her spiritual importance—a person due respect. That's why he absconded into that house. Augusta Bolte now knew what she wanted. She jumped out of the car, slammed the door shut and ran into—i.e., she wanted to run.

"Stop!" yelled the driver,[23] "first pay!"—Augusta looked for her handbag and didn't find it. Suddenly a saving thought came to her, given that she had always already been a brilliantined girl, even back in school. She described to the chauffeur the corner on which she had put down her handbag way back when she had pursued those 5 persons on foot and had needed to jettison ballast, and told him that there was more money in the handbag

[23] Like the author himself.

than he had asked for and that he should keep the rest as a tip. The man became enraged and used the term "swindler" to describe her. In answer, Miss Dr. Augusta insisted that she was true and real and fighting for idealism; she wanted to be the first one to receive a Dr. Lif.—"What" asked the driver, "an olive? Nonsense Augusta—marry you musta!" and reminded her one more time to pay in cash. Miss Dr. Prof. Lif insistently presented the carman with the fact that she had to get out of the car. Here the decision would fall, here she would reap the fruits of her studies, she had to reach the man who had absconded into that house, in order to ask him what he really wanted. The driver asked again and again for his money by moving his hand like an oaktree in a storm. She only talked about idealism. Now the driver thought she was crazy and became afraid of her.

Suddenly the driver grabbed Miss Dr. Liverwurst[24] with both hands, set her down in the car, without worrying about her screaming, and drove away. He drove and he drove until the car reached a large sandy place on the moor. He stopped in the middle of a giant military training area, deposited Miss Dr. Augusta, and drove away.

The reader might have thought that something would be happening here; maybe that the troops would have arrived. But the troops didn't arrive, did not find Miss Dr. Lif and didn't get any pleasure out of this flower. Maybe the reader would have thought that Miss Dr. Lif would have starved to death here, but she didn't starve. Maybe the reader would have thought that Miss Dr. Lif would find her way back home like a cat; but she didn't find it. Certainly the reader will think that Miss Dr. Lif would find out who or what is going on, but she finds out nothing. The reader believes that he has the right to find out, but the reader has no right, and certainly not the right to find out anything in a work of art. Certainly the reader has an inkling that here Miss Dr. Augusta will be recompensed for her efforts, maybe that the rector of the university will come and make her a full Professor of Lif. Nope.

It's just that the story is over, simply over, no matter how sorry I am, no matter how brutal it must sound, there's nothing else I

[24]Respectively liver extract.

can do. I, as the author, state here that this is the conclusion of my attempt to offer an Augusta Bolte to the people. Many thanks!

    Einbeck, 1. 7. 1922   Merz

POSTSCRIPT
The hammer already hovers, the catastrophe approaches.
                                           (Rector Lauenstein.)

PJ

circa 1923   **Shepherd's Play**

THE LITTLE SHEPHERDESS
                    Here I be feeding my sheepeepeep. *Looks around, once to the right, once to the left.*
SHEPHERDESS   Here I be feeding my sheepeepeep. *Looks around a long time.*
SHEPHERDESS   Whaaat?
                    Here I be feeding my sheepeepeep.
                    My sheepeepeep
                    sheepeepeep.
                    yawns Yuck, if this isn't boring!
                    jumps up, dances, sings tralala tiederallala tralalalala!
                    pause
                    Here I be feeding my sheepeepeep.
                    No one coming?
                    Oh yeah.
                    My sheepeepeep.
                    Little Rascal comes in.
RASCAL   Good morning.
SHEPHERDESS   Good morning.
                    pause
RASCAL   Cantcha give us a curtsey?
SHEPHERDESS   Don't got the time.
RASCAL   Whatcha so busy with?
SHEPHERDESS   Here I be feeding my sheepeepeep.
RASCAL   I hope you enjoy it.
SHEPHERDESS   You call this enjoyment?
RASCAL   You don't want to do it, or what?
SHEPHERDESS   Aw, what would you know from it?
RASCAL   More than you would!
SHEPHERDESS   Aw, get outta here.
RASCAL   Then give 's a curtsey.
SHEPHERDESS   *curtseys* I be here feeding my sheepeepeep.
RASCAL   Be quiet.
SHEPHERDESS   *curtseys* I be here feeding my sheepeepeep.
RASCAL   You, shut your mouth!
SHEPHERDESS   *curtseys* I be here feeding my sheepeepeep.
RASCAL   I'll bash your head in.

SHEPHERDESS	*curtseys* I be here feeding my sheepeepeep.
RASCAL	Listen, girlie.
SHEPHERDESS	*curtseys* I be here feeding my sheepeepeep.
RASCAL	*raises a fist* You better shut up.
SHEPHERDESS	*curtseys* I be here feeding my sheepeepeep.
RASCAL	*hits her* Take that . . . and that.
SHEPHERDESS	*yowling and laughing* 'Cause I'm minding my sheep?
RASCAL	You just shut up!
	pause
RASCAL	Now what?
	pause
RASCAL	Say something!
	pause
RASCAL	Say something!
SHEPHERDESS	*curtseys* I be here——feeding——my sheepeepeep.
RASCAL	Listen, girlie!
SHEPHERDESS	*takes her sheep and slowly goes off with them* I be here feeding my sheepeepeep.

JR

circa 1925 **Shadow Play**

CHARACTERS
ELENA, the young woman
LAURA, a young man's fancy
FRIEDRICH, Laura's maker
EMIL, the other man, Friedrich's friend
LIME, Emil's shadow

1.
The shadow play stage is empty, now enter from the left:
a head
a foot
a hand
an arm } *they assemble themselves into the*
a skirt } *young woman and step forward*
a blouse
another foot

LAURA — I am Laura. I am a young man's fancy. I was born out of a young man's fancy.

2.
ELENA — *from the left.* What's going on? Who's here?
LAURA — My name is Laura. I was born out of a young man's fancy.
ELENA — What's the man called?
LAURA — Friedrich. And what are you called?
ELENA — I am—I am not only called, I *am* Elena. But PHOO on you for being born out of a young man's fancy. And PHOO on the man from whose fancy only a girl can be born.
LAURA — And who are you to get so riled up about it?
ELENA — A genuine woman. Which means I'll scratch your eyes out, little witch. Why can't a guy like that end up with me instead? I yearn until my soul is black and blue, and Friedrich cooks a woman up out of his fancy. A Laura.
LAURA — Because you women aren't good enough for all these spoiled men. You aren't smart enough for anyone who's got a brain. Just look at me: a model for all women, exactly what a woman ought to be.

ELENA	You nervy slut you, you male phantasy! What kind of talk is that against a decent woman! Just clear out!
LAURA	*I* have as much right to be here as you. You scarecrow!
ELENA	We'll see about that! Pack your bones up in a box and ship your soul to Friedrich! *Shakes Laura, who falls apart, and throws the parts over the right side of the stage.* There.

3.

LIME	*enters from the left, stops. Elena looks at him with fascination.* My name is Lime.
ELENA	O, you sweetheart! Are you the product of a *woman's* fancy?
LIME	No way. I am an honest to goodness shadow. I am the shadow of a man.
ELENA	And what's the man doing without his shadow?
LIME	He's looking around for me until his eyes go blind, because he misses me so much.
ELENA	Come over here and sit down next to me. Let's talk about why he misses you so much. *Sits down.*
LIME	Because he can't live without his shadow. *Sits down too.* The spot where I broke off is really painful for him.
ELENA	Poor guy. Is it Friedrich?
LIME	No, it's Emil. And I was his trusty shadow long enough.
ELENA	Gee, you sure are heartless, but I also really think you're great.
LIME	Why shouldn't a shadow have a heart?
ELENA	Kiss me!
LIME	O, you sweetheart!
ELENA	I've never seen a man like this shadow.
LIME	*kisses her.* I love you. We will be faithful to each other, Elena.
ELENA	O, what a lot of class this guy has, what a lot of swank. Is there a guy that's sweller than this shadow?

4.

FRIEDRICH	*enters from the left.* My name is Friedrich. *Stops.* Friedrich is my name! What's this I see?
LIME	Whatever it is, you're wrong!
FRIEDRICH	This is the shadow of my friend Emil, who's miserably been looking for him thirteen days already.
ELENA	I swear to God, he's as much a trueblue gent as you are.

FRIEDRICH	I'll bet you this one is no gent because this one in fact is Emil's shadow. Who *are* you, Mister Shadow?
LIME	That is kind of hard to say.
FRIEDRICH	Come on, no excuses now, who are you?
LIME	Honor bright, I'm nothing, just a name.
FRIEDRICH	"I'm nothing"? Shadows are nothing too. What's your name then?
LIME	Lime.
FRIEDRICH	Lime? That's nothing but Emil spelled backward. Now hear me out. I don't recognize any name like Lime. I'm telling you straight to your shadow head, you are Emil's shadow, nothing but.
ELENA	O Lime, run off—but come right back.
FRIEDRICH	*I'm* going to bring poor Emil here right now. So he can take his shadow back. And you, Mister Lime, you just wait for us here!
LIME	What's it your business, huh. Don't say I didn't warn you. *Shoots at Friedrich, without hitting him. Runs off to the right.*
FRIEDRICH	*runs after him.* You dirty bum, watch out!

5.

EMIL	*from the left.* Loveliest, daintiest, and charmingest lady, my name is Emil.
ELENA	O what a classy way to say hello!
EMIL	Didn't I just hear my friend Friedrich here?
ELENA	You don't have to be in such a hurry, mister, he went by here a long time ago.
EMIL	You see in me a broken man, my shadow broken off from me. I am looking for my shadow, which is mine all mine.
ELENA	I know your shadow, who is such a handsome gent.
EMIL	WHERE is he?
ELENA	*distracting him.* Ah, but you're a thousand times more handsome than your shadow!
EMIL	Horsefeathers! Well? My shadow, where's my shadow? Without my shadow I'm like half a man. Can half a man be any kind of handsome?
ELENA	You're pretty neat even without your shadow.
EMIL	I've got such pains here on this spot where my shadow broke off. I can't live without my shadow.

ELENA	You poor exhausted man!
EMIL	And worries! Who knows what dumb things my shadow might cook up without me. Like getting married. O what a miserable man I surely am!
ELENA	THIS guy's only concern is for his shadow. Aw gee, I wish I was his shadow.
EMIL	Where is my shadow?
ELENA	Go out and find your shadow. *Pointing to the right.* See, there's where your shadow ran away to.
EMIL	THAT good for nothing bum! *Exits to the right.*

6.

ELENA	He loves me not, only his shadow loves me. He doesn't, not once, look at me.
LAURA	*from right, running.* Help, a man is chasing me.
LIME	*enters from the right, running right in back of Laura.* Take it easy, little girl, I can't run as fast as you, because I'm just a shadow.
LAURA	Help me, Elena, you're my friend!
ELENA	O LIME, you dirty double-dealer! And you, you floozy, Laura, only existing as a thought in some guy's brain. I won't help you, just you see the way I'll help you.
LAURA	But don't you see, I'm not a young man's fancy any more. Now I'm an honest to goodness woman. Otherwise this Lime guy wouldn't chase me.
ELENA	I hate you. Do you think I'd help you when you take my sweetie from me?
LAURA	I'm not doing anything, it's him that's chasing *me.*
LIME	O both of you dear darling girls, I love you both. Won't you both be my darling little wives?

7.

FRIEDRICH	Wasn't Lime just here? Where's he gone off to? But look, here's little Laura.
LAURA	Help, help! Where should I hide? The shadow is wearing me down, and then this man here tears me into pieces with his looks.
FRIEDRICH	Laura, you creature of my fancy, you my soul, you one and only woman whom I love, I love you!
LAURA	O, save me, I'm dying beneath his stronger gaze.

FRIEDRICH	I love this dear head on its slender neck, this black hair like the sea at night. O were it only mine!
LAURA	*During the following she slowly falls apart, the pieces disappearing into or in back of Friedrich.* O, my poor head! *Her head flies to the back of Friedrich's head.*
FRIEDRICH	And o these gentle slender hands, and these fine arms, o were they mine!
LAURA	O, my hands, my arms. *As above.*
FRIEDRICH	And o this dainty little foot! O were it mine!
LAURA	O, my poor foot! *It disappears, as before.*
FRIEDRICH	And these well-developed limbs, this lovely form, o were they mine!
LAURA	*disappears completely behind Friedrich, except a single foot.* O, my poor limbs!
FRIEDRICH	But Laura, where are you, Laura? O, my girl! I only see a single foot here.
ELENA	Dummy! She's with you now! You wished her up into yourself!
FRIEDRICH	I'm miserable! What am I going to do now with a single foot?
LIME	Elena, you fairest of all ladies, now I love but you. Just listen to me!
ELENA	Not so fast now, sweetheart! You're being lovey dovey now that Laura's gone away. But before now you were out to really land her.
LIME	Listen to me. Now I only have a few moments left to live, I'm fading fast.
ELENA	Then come here, sweetie, and climb into my arms.
FRIEDRICH	What I have to see and suffer through! All I have left of my wife is a single foot, and now this hotdog here, who is only a shadow, the shadow of my friend, an empty shadow, lies here in the arms of a swell lady, who says she loves him.
ELENA	Then bug off, Friedrich, there's no woman here who loves you.
FRIEDRICH	Not on your sweet life. I'm going to kill this shadow here and now. *Goes at Lime with a knife.*

8.

EMIL	*enters quickly from the right.* Take it easy, friend. YOU'LL kill me too if you kill my shadow.

ELENA	Leave *me* the shadow.
EMIL	No, he's mine. How can I leave him to you? But if you would be mine, Lime would also be thine.
ELENA	O, aren't you swell, and you're even better looking than this shadow. I love you just as much as I love him.
EMIL	Well, you're swell too. And I love you with all the passion in my soul.
LIME	And I love you too, just like the apple of my eye.
EMIL	So come on, Lime, dear shadow, the both of us are still just one. Let's reunite ourselves. You'll be my shadow once again, and then we'll love Elena in common.
LIME	Great. I'll be your shadow like before. So, shove me in.
	He steps close to Emil, who shoves him in, and he once again becomes a shadow.
FRIEDRICH	And what am I supposed to do here?
ELENA	Well, you still have Laura's foot, so take it home with you.
FRIEDRICH	Come on, foot, this is no place for us to stay. *Exits to left with foot.*
ELENA	Okay now, both my loves, Emil and Lime, man and shadow, come now to your darling Elena.
EMIL	Most honored lady, I and my shadow wait here at your bidding.
	He kisses her, then steps a little to the side, his shadow rises up and also kisses her.

JR

1928   **Profane Words over the Eternal City**

A view—
I'm always on Michelangelo's trail.
A view as if from the Eiffel tower.
If only one could still get tea!
Yack, how profane, the only thing missing in Saint Peter's is
   the Blackbottom, and the bar'd be ready.
Down there one can buy good picture postcards for one mark,
   6 by 9.
If you look through there, you'll see the Pantheon.
Such a small staircase. One should measure how small
   staircases can be.
It will get better.
You have to wait, there's a lady up there, she has trouble
   squeezing through.
So what can you see in the cupola?
Nothing, but one has to have been up there.
The heat up there fa troppo caldo.
Please, you may climb up, if you think you can squeeze
   through.
This heat's unbearable.
The dome of Saint Peter's! Many a pope has never been here.
But on the way out, one has to tip.
5 cents is enough, the man down there wants to see goodwill.
That in Italy people always demand tips, even in Saint Peter's.
National habit.
In Paris they call it pourboire.
I find that it profanes the beautiful church.
But that's their job.
Above all, watch out for pickpockets!
My notebook was stolen in the dome.
Let's hope nobody lops the dome off right now!
The gentleman also found it enormously hot up here.
Everyone's bound to find that.
The town hall in Hannover is only one quarter as high.
Then it doesn't need to be propped up.
If you whisper here, you can hear it very clearly over there.

Do you think he had started to saw into that?
But of course, why else would the knife be lying there?
I'm not asking, I just wanted to check if you could hear me.
You don't say! Perfectly!
It was hot up there in the cupola!
Very hot.
One can also whisper in the Kreuzkirche in Dresden, it also works in the baroque.
What do you mean?
I mean that he has started to saw into it.
Amazing that the mosaics don't disturb the whispering any more than they do!
The whisper sums it up.
Zeiss in Jena would build this whole dome only 10 centimeters thick.
The trick is in the shotcrete!
That's why one can only build profane buildings today.
You still hear me?
Keep on whispering.
There was a girl up in the cupola who was wearing lace panties, how unmodern.
Don't whisper so loud, the lady's standing next to me.
But pretty they were!
You can't please everybody.
From up here one can see very well that the lateral façade walls aren't always necessary.
Do you believe that the new architecture can do completely without decorative walls?
Beauty lies in the form, not in decoration or perspective.
That's something to be remembered.
Anyway, how do you dare even mention a railway station in Saint Peter's?
Our age knows only the functional building.
Just think, Saint Peter's church is the biggest church in the world!
Do you see the cat walking on the roof over there?
In Rome cats are dogs.
But they don't bark.

But they smell like dogs.
They keep the mice out of the churches.
If only one could drive one's car directly to Saint Peter's!
What would Mai have to say about Saint Peter's?
He would say: "The trees are coming into leaf!"
In Rome a development like that in Frankfurt is completely inconceivable.
Frankfurt has Mai, Rome has the tradition.
And that poor pope who can't leave his garden for the rest of his life!
On the other hand, nobody else is allowed in.
But what if he ever wanted to get out?
To get to the Castel Sant'Angelo the pope uses a hidden pathway similar to the roman waterpipes.
E vietato scrivere.
After all Saint Peter's church is not a lookout tower.
The only problem is, one gets too little sleep in Rome.
One doesn't need to be Catholic at all to understand that.
Believe you me, in the old days the pope was the ruler of the world.
The interior is truly a first-class architectural design.
Don't you really mean its height?
No, I know it's 53 meters to the first circular corridor in the dome, I paid 50 cents to know.
The diameter is 40 meters.
More important for me is the mastery of the composition.
What do you mean by that? One can never see the whole space at once.
The large stripes see to that.
The design of the altar niche is a painterly-architectonic masterpiece.
How come?
Do you see how the rays emanating from the dove are arrested by the bodies and on the other hand are transmitted to the architecture?
Just between us, but the human body is finally an incredibly abstract form.
The style of the tabernacle is fantastic!

They wanted to imitate the columns of the temple in Jerusalem.
The tabernacle and stairs leading down to the Sacred Grotto are grotesque.
It functions as counterpoint to the renaissance of the church.
By the way, one isn't allowed to use the stairs that lead to the crypt.
In the Sancta Veronica you go down for 2 lira.
You'd need to stand nearly 40 men on top of each other, just to reach the ceiling of the nave.
Permesso, Signore!
Stop running around in front of the praying women!
Foreshortening is the joke of architecture, perspective is a bad joke.
You wouldn't be a Bolshevik, would you?
Why?
Because you always have such bizarre brainstorms.
How even a little sun structures the room so very naturally!
One should study history, or have you perchance seen the film *Il re dei re*?
Magnificent, like the best Russian films.
Faith is still a very powerful thing.
How daring to put Christ in a film!
One knows him otherwise only as sculpture or painting.
Here he becomes a man like us, you experience his humanity.
It reminded me of my childhood.
Those lovely, pious stories of the healing of the sick and the painful passion.
Look at it, this door is opened only once every 25 years in a special ceremony.
He who doesn't have any worries, will worry about that.
Now it's bricked over.
Do you believe that that's piety?
I just can't believe that that's what Christ wanted.
It is only ritual.
They could just as well have bricked over the other door.
The mores of different countries are different.
It depends on the needs of the people.

You're mistaken, humans all have the same needs.
But different peoples have different needs.
The different needs of the peoples are artificial, not artistic.
The most important thing is if one has lost the war or not.
Perspective is as much of a fakery in the life of a people as in architecture.
Like representation in painting.
Where there's faith, every fakery takes root.
Yack, how godless!
How small the cupola looks from outside, and yet there were ten of us inside.
Don't forget the girl with the lace panties.
Just imagine it from down here!
She was certainly not an Englishwoman.
Just how come all the most beautiful places in the world are ruined by shopkeepers?
By sandwich papers and graffiti, and even by glee clubs.
The shopkeepers also want to live.
One can never find what one needs, but junk one doesn't need is always on offer.
It's called industry.
If my gray pants weren't torn, I could spare my good blue suit.
That one's forced to live so economically!
I'd like to be able to make do with 22 lira a day.
That's about 5 marks, that should be possible.
I'm a well-known artist, that's another reason why I have to live economically.
The experience is independent of the quantity of money one spends.
Subsistence level.
Seen from up front, St. Peter's looks like a set.
That's the work of perspective, may God's grace be with it.
Do you hear the screeching of the trolley?
Just as in Halle, every time it turns a corner.
Oggetti Religiosi.
In this shop the pious Christians buy stuff when they don't know what to do with their feelings.
There's one shop next to the other near Saint Peter's.

Industry wants to live too!
I wonder if the shopkeepers are also pious Christians?
These here macaronis are absolutely first class.
Completely devoid of perspective, only functional design.
And look here at all those sugar-lambs with crosses on their breasts.
The banner reads Buona Pasque.
At one lira 50 a lamb like that is cheaper than visiting the Sacred Grotto.
But there are bigger ones too.
For 3 lira you can even get a kilo of the finest quality prunes.
You're plum funny.
Sinite parvulos venire ad me.
The Tiber is just as yellow as the Leine.
There are also daisies near the Castel Sant'Angelo.
But the Tiber is a slightly lighter yellow.
What do you want with the Tiber, I didn't come to Rome to look at dirty water.
It's due to the loamy bottom.
I don't want to know about loam, what interests me are the ruins.
Loamy soil makes work difficult for the farmers. Animal fertilizer breaks it down.
Why don't you shut up!
Why did the old Romans build so many ruins?
You're mistaken, back then they were spick-and-span and smoothly polished. It's the climate.
We're dealing here with the beauty of Rome, which supposedly is greater than that of other cities.
Why did you come to Rome anyway?
To ascertain this.
You see the cabdriver with the large umbrella.
Well, it's raining!
It smells like lions here, but they were only cats.
That's modern Italy.
What do you think of Mussolini?
Rome will never be New York.
Obviously.

My hat's as wet as back then in Paris.
This is the Forum? Why is it so broken down?
The tooth of time.
Here's a warehouse. How large Wertheim is!
Il Gesù, the most important church after Saint Peter's.
Baroque, like Hildesheim.
Have you heard about the Italia Ungheria football match?
I'm against sports. I don't care who wins, someone always does.
That's true, why should one get upset?
And the antiquities?
Does stampe really mean mailbox?
Why?
Because it always looks so red.
Do you see, that woman's mouth is always wide open.
What does it mean, ways———open—?
It's because she can't close it, her upper lip's become too short.
You mean *is*, it can't really have become short, if it was long enough.
Of course, birth defect.
In Rome!
L'Italia di domani.
Il leva fascista—Marcelleria
Bar
Bar in Italian means a very small saloon.
Tabacchi
Orlogheria
The large staircase here.
No good for cars.
This eternal rain . . .
This eternal Rome!
Just remember Gelsenkirchen for once!
The Hans Sachs house, painted by Michelangelo . . .
God save us, only furnished by Doctor Max Burchartz.
Isn't that the one from Essen?
Contradictions—Believe it or not, but from outside I don't think that Saint Peter's is even beautiful.
You narrow-minded philistine.

Would you like to buy good plums, 40 cents apiece?
Signore, dove è il Forum.
Grazie, Signorina.
Dictralà.
How the monks walk barefoot.
Though in sandals.
Earlier, earlier, earlier— —
Later, later, later— —
Rome—
New York—
Hannover?
Some never learn.
Today we're happy that we've got at least these remains.
At the old Forum they now dry the laundry.
Sono Italiana?
Si, e Lei?
Tedesco.
Prego, prego.
Excuse me, did you step on my foot?
I mistook it for an excavation, please forgive me.
Thank you, I just wanted to tell you, if I want to go on, you can just stay here.
I have never seen the least drop of rain in Rome.
With all the stuff that surfaces here, one can't open one's eyes wide enough to take it all in.
Would you care to always live among ruins?
Why ever did the old Romans build so many ruins?
As you all know, that's the Titus Arch.
Titus destroyed Jerusalem, as everyone knows.
One can explain it only that way, although it isn't true in fact.
You've missed the most beautiful things, they're back there.
I'm looking for my sweet Greek virgin, whom I love so much.
Phidias, no need for commentaries.
The dancing maenad—
A priestess who has come in heat and who in trance is looking for the godhead.
This afternoon at 3:00, Palazzo Doria!
Si prego di non toccare.

The most important thing, when contemplating ancient art, is
   to see how one may no longer do it, to see which worldview
   is over and done with for good.
Each era has its own forms of expression.
The form of the Romans was crude.
Architects they were, however.
Clarity in arrangement in architecture and integration of the
   painting—One must never let oneself be misled by erosion.
Or through fake reconstruction in favor of the object.
Imagination always completes completely.
Criticism breaks everything down.
They had a knack for the portrait.
For ladies too?
How beat these horses are!
Where's your hair, August, August?
The same hit songs as in Germany.
No, in Germany they're already passé.
Do you know what this is? This is ancient medicine.
No, those are votive gifts.
Aphrodite Anadyomene.
Nascita di Aphrodite.
That's the Aphrodite of Venus.
Voyez la volupture, comme ça . . .
A true Venus, when a girl can love as well as this stone figure.
A bit on the cold side.
But the expression . . .
I like plump women.
A slim figure is always cold.
C'est l'expression de la bouche, elle respire l'odeur de la vie.
Miss, you may confidently stand next to the Venus of
   Aphrodite, she pales next to you.
The poor lady turned beet red!———
Mussolini was some guy!
Still is.
These doodads were fixed in front of the boat.
That's for eternity.
By the way, the Venus of Aphrodite is a truly dumb joke.
Nothing escapes you!

Why is it a dumb joke?
Because it has to be Aphrodite of Venus, of course.
So what's dumb now?
The joke.
I'm too stupid, can't see the joke.
Joker!
The animal, just look at the expression on its face!
That's a bed, over there, in the middle.
It's a tester bed.
No, it's a couch.
Did the old Romans already have couches?
For industry.
This is the highpoint of Greek naturalism, tamed only by a figleaf.
After Alexander the Great it becomes manneristic.
The officer we saw yesterday looked the same.
You can only appreciate the truly good, when you can label the less good as exactly that.
It is important to avoid fakery in art.
Euripides, the classic Dadaist.
Dadaists existed at all times.
In questo locale non si parla di politica.
In the papal art gallery the WC carries the beautifully ornate inscription "Rhine."
Concession to Germany.
Germany's river, not its borders.
Here is the Piazza del Popolo.
Sometimes however there's a lot of fakery in architecture.
Shouldn't be!
Fakery always takes revenge.
And a letter from Luther was consciously laid next to the letters by Dante, Petrarch, etc.
Castiglione il Cortegliano.
Ex munificentia Pii X.
Unerringly misfired.
The Romans were simply a crude merchant people.
And totally kitschy.
The famous prince sent to Rome with the mission to be poisoned by the pope.

Which he promptly didn't do.
Can allegory properly also be art?
Art has nothing to do with art.
Ouch, that's an old joke that has nothing to do with a joke.
Allegory has nothing to do with allegory.
He who has nothing to do, does that.
He who has no worries, has nothing to do with art.
There's that silly old roman couch again.
No, it ain't!
Why's that bed in a glass cage?
O God, this beautiful Niobe here, I don't even have it as a postcard.
They'll have given you a ward, Miss.
What are all these papers doing here?
Today's Mardi Gras, remember.
And it doesn't stop raining.
Fachino, polire le Scarpe!
Andiamo!
Grazie.
Prego!
How sweet Victor Emanuel's monument is!
A gauche de la Piazza Doria.
But nobody hit upon the idea of including the donkey in the world of music, the animal's surprised.
Grünewald's Christ lies the other way round.
What a saucy image!
It is matter become spirit.
Christian bones.
Me too, I'm going to take along one of those Christian bones from the catacombs.
They're refilled twice a year.
Mine's brittle already.
It really is quite impossible to live among all this junk.
Piazza Barberina?
In fondo a destra.
Foot ball.
Banco di Santo Spirito.
English Warehouse.

Football, football, football.
And here once again, the silly old roman couch under glass.
Got nothing to do with allegory.
One can't open one's eyes wide enough.
The form of the Romans was crude.
But they were architects.
I like plump women.
A slim figure is always cold.
The Venus of Aphrodite again, a Konrad joke.
You're mistaking my foot for an excavation again?
How come?
How come, how goes, you goose, you've stepped on it again.
Permesso.
Birth defect, of course.
Ugh, how godless!
The experience is independent of the quantity of money one spends.
Have you already been in the cupola?
For hours.
Lire 30, l'etto.
Piano, piano.
Pianoforte.
We have a Steinway grand at home.
Do you know the pictures of V. Freno?
Monsieur Bragaglia n'est pas ici.
Rupe Tarpea.
Osteria.
Alleatico Pantelleria.
And we had thought we'd see all this in the sun.
The shadow of a tired old horse remains a tired old horse.
And the shadow of an art is kitsch.
Remains art.
And the shadow of Rome is still and always a Rome.
This palm tree reminds me of Rio.
Oh, have you been there?
No, how about you?
How can the palm tree remind you of something you don't know?

From the movies.
You know your way around.
Si scende avanti.
In Italy, one gets on the trolley in back and out in front.
This is the house where Napoleon's mother lived.
Here every house has a cat.
Pantelleria, that's even further south than Sicily, you can't find that wine anywhere.
Am I seeing double, or are there 2 churches over there?
No, that's a tangle of 2 churches.
Down here it's roasted on the spit.
Mistrust yourself to the utmost degree, one has the right to err and to revoke.
Capella Sistina.
A waterfall.
Heap of rubble.
Do you see the face of Michelangelo?
He has eternalized himself in that bearskin.
Has the bearskin now become art?
You just have to know it.
The complete process of the birth of a human being, plastically represented in marble.
That's why we got so hot while running.
Do you know Karl Heinz Munz?
No, did he also paint in the chapel?
No, but he's done a portrait of me.
It's a pity that Michelangelo's works are so high up that one can't see them with the naked eye.
All you need are stronger binoculars.
It's truly an incredible pity that all these artists have always had to work for an apple and a piece of bread.
The same's true today, dear lady!
I've got it all down pat now.
You should still go and visit the Pantheon, it's open until noon.
My neck's so stiff, I can't turn it anymore.
Art can never stand still and it's always been that way.
Even as it wants to follow the inner being, it has to move forward.

Art means to create.
Art's got nothing to do with crates.
Another Konrad joke!
Here you see Apollo. His only clothing is a figleaf.
This god over here is small, elegant, and naked.
Clothes make the man.
You cannot live forever in pathos.
Some never get there.
I can exactly recognize your back directly.
End.
Eternal cities also have an end.
Profane words over eternal cities have to come to an end.
As long as there will be eternal cities, there will be profane words over them.

PJ

1929   **In the Middle of the World a House Stands**
       Sketch for a Movie

   1) In the middle of a meadow there's a
      little house and outside the window
      in the virginia creepers
      there's a little bird's nest.

   2) And behind the curtains
      there's a young girl dreaming.
      There's a girl who dreams
      of love and happy days.
      In dreams.

   3) Then a bird taps on her window.
      Can you help me?
      Bird comes flying in.
      A letter: Loved one, come to her who loves you.
      The bird has taken the letter and flown
      far over the ocean and
      over the flowering land
      and has found
      a profoundly . . . pale youth.
      He is reading her letter.

   4) He has written his answer:
      A letter: I come to you!
      The bird brought it back to her.
      The man headed off on his travels.
      The girl wrote him back, the bird turned
      around, found his flat standing vacant, a cat
      ate the bird.

      Misfortunes and traumas, joys and desires,
      till he finally finds her.
      In the meantime she had sent the bird back,
      but the bird still hadn't found him. She unconsolable.

a
He gets in an auto, starts driving. Streets, houses, skyscrapers, landscapes, he's driving. Birds flying by him. He's driving. A lake. Seagulls soar down. A young girl. On the shore a young girl, he climbs out, asks her a question, moves on, empty environs, small cottage, he knocks, spends the night there.

Break-in in his office, things stolen.

His car is stolen by bandits.

His business burns up.

A girl wakes up in the cottage and stares at him. She looks scared, then bewildered, then happy, comes over, is stroking the sleeper, tucking him in.

Morning. Waking up, blankets? The young girl comes in, brings him milk. He thanks her and drinks, wants to go. She takes her driver's license and goes with him. In the forest, trees. In back of the trees

b
She loses him, she turns back.
A railroad freight car he boards—between crates—is discovered—one of them wants to throw him off—another one puts him to work—A station—he makes his escape.

Begs for handouts for food, young girl in auto picks him up—takes care of him—

He stays for days, weeks, works, is silent. She is speaking, he isn't.

Evening—moon—garden—he and she—he is talking—she strokes him—

c
He talks about his work, how he was rich, how well his business worked for him, how he was spoiled by women, how his life

sickened him, how the bird tapped at his window, brought him a letter, how he answered, how the bird flew back and forth and vanished, how he was left alone. How he took off.

She strokes and comforts him. Again he longs to wander.

II. Cut
She travels with him overseas. Big ship, ocean liner. Dances. Games. Baths. They sail past cities—mountains—islands—into port. They spend a few days in the port. Then they travel to a first-class spa. She's thrilled to be near him, before his eyes he sees the image of a virgin. She tries to talk him into something, he misunderstands her; sees her only as a stranger. In the night he runs away.

She searches for him in his room, in the park, no one knows where he's run off to. She contacts the authorities, gets them to join the search. Autos and bicyclists in all directions, searching.

He wanders over country roads. A biker spots him, stops him, rides on, telephones her.

She hops in a car, catches up with him. They go by car through valleys ringed by snowy mountains, sometimes stop at gorges, waterfalls, high pastures, in low country.

Empty moors. Clouds.
Clouds.

Birch trees   Birch galleries   A crossroads. He has her pull over. He splits from her, kisses her forehead, thanks her, now he takes off. She watches him go, she stands still, climbs into car, doesn't follow, stays on, still stays on, still watches him. Now it grows dark.

d
So he came to that same neighborhood and
wandered on that moor to that same hut, where he imagined that the girl that he had dreamed about was waiting, whom he loved.
He comes, stares deeply at her, she at him, they interchange deep stares, reach out their hands, they laugh, he lifts her high, he takes her in his arms and kisses her.

And they began to talk and didn't understand each other's talk because they both talked different.
And he was stunned to see it wasn't that same girl who wrote the letter to him, about whom he dreamed.
They looked at each other stunned, he squeezed her hand.

And so they split again, and he came back to that same crossroads.
Kisses her forehead and makes his way back to the
crossroads, where the car with the other one is still waiting. She's overjoyed to be with him again, he comes up, hugs and kisses her.

So did he give his life's companion her first kiss.

We watch them drive the whole way back, from there to that same giant city where his offices, his factory, had been. He finds it all destroyed and plundered, all burnt down.

Factories and workers, giving him a last hurrah.

JR

1929   **Two Choruses from *Above and Below***

Chorus I
For Moving Speech Choir

At the beginning the stage is dark blue. It looks empty because one cannot see the people lying on the floor. Vaguely at first, then with growing clarity one sees against this backdrop, the orbiting of worlds, spheres, that turn, lit up in red, green, and blue, transparent circles, lines, before all parabolic forms, sparkling lines, squares that contract and expand, yellow or red, and in between foggy forms, irregular veils in front of the mathematical shapes.... The monotone of a foghorn comes in at intervals. At times one also hears the roar of water. Short shrill sound of a high-pitched whistle. The clanking of glass shards. A large red sphere, becoming gradually brighter, rises and disappears, while a siren wails. Immediately afterward a spotlight begins to light up those areas of the stage where there are no people.

VOICES FROM OUTSIDE
Nothing.
Nighten.
Nothing.
Dampen.
Drone.
Weave veil.
Without.
Ur-eternal.
Limit.
Infinite thousandfold null.
Nothing,
Nighten,
Null.

Nighten	nothing
Nothing	nothing
Dampen	nothing
Drone	nothing
Weave veil	nothing
Without	strive
Ur-eternal	strive
Limit	strive

Infinite thousand- times null	strive	
Nothing	strive	
Nighten	nothing	
Null	infinite	
Nighten		
Dampen	nighten	
Weave veil	nighten	
Without		
Nothing without limit eternal nighten		nighten
Infinite thousandfold nighten		nighten
Null nighten nighten nighten		nighten
Night nighten nighten nighten		nighten
Nothing nighten nighten nighten		nighten
Null nothing null nothing null nothing null nothing		
Null		
Null		
Null		

While speaking, flat bowls shine through the backdrop and flatten and foreshorten themselves. At "ur-eternal" a cross. Everything transparent. People on stage invisible: Being is hidden.

CHOIR		Nighten nighten nighten
	Giants thousand millions	Nighten nighten nighten
	Billions thousand trillions	Nighten nighten nighten
	Zillions eternal burn drone	Nighten nighten nighten
	Afloat veil	Nighten nighten
	Float	Veil
	Winds	Veil
	Light dark winds veil	Grasp veil

A pale light comes on; one recognizes shadowy human figures.

Grasp giants thousand thousand	Nighten nighten
And want to grasp grasp grasp	Null null

	And burst break shards shards	Null null
	And want want want	Want want
	And make poems grasp float reach	Want want
	And make poems think create speak	Want want
	And whirl break dare	Want want
	Light! *The light turns dawny.*	
	And grow give limp turn	Want want
	And sink bed root stand	Want want
	And dare peak blow go	Want want
	Light!! *Loudly—it becomes lighter*	
	We are becoming.	
	We feel.	
	We can.	
	Light!!! *Louder—it becomes even lighter*	
HUMANS		Want want
		softly
	And ball sink float carry	Humans Humans
		softly
	And stand go reach dare	Humans Humans
		softly
	And create grasp bed root	Humans Humans
		softly
HUMANS		Humans Humans
	Blind?	Nighten nighten
	<u>May God give us light!!!!</u> *It becomes quite light.*	

Chorus II

GROUP 2   O what misery, you up there Above
             You stomp our rights into the ground!
             We were denied justice!
             Bandits, murderers! Poison and hell!
             Ore resounds crazed lament,
             Daring thirsts over shards,
             Dirth-death, hesitate,
             Three hundred sixty-five days,
             Cold little brother fish,
             Mute friends svelte,

Light shines shiny scales,
Your body and your soul, svelte,
Your vile mouth slurps waterwaves,
Your little hands splash above,
Below,
Humid,
Water in water,
You and us;
Below,
Where the deep wets
Your body silvers,
The waves your chirping.
To bathe,
To bathe,
<u>To bathe the little fish!!!</u>

GROUP 1	Strength powers blocks iron steel,	
	Stepped-on bell to heat siren roars;	
	The hammer wops thunderclap,	
	Lightning flashes iron swords sparks tank,	
	Lightning flashes bomb ignites howls and hisses.	
	Turbine machine iron cement	
	Wheels pistons concrete	
	Turbine machine iron cement	
	Smelting towers coal engine	
	Turbine machine iron cement	GROUP 2
	Flywheels	Turn turn
	Turbine machine iron cement	
	Smelting towers	Turn turn
	Engines howl	Turn turn
	Canons blast	Turn turn
	Turbine machine iron cement	
	Wheels pistons concrete	
	Turbine machine iron cement	
	Smelting towers coal engine	
	Turbine machine iron cement	
	Wheels	Screech screech
	Turbine machine iron cement	

Smelting towers	Screech screech
Engines howl	Screech screech
Canons blast	Screech screech
	Howl howl
	Screech screech
	Blast blast
	Turn turn
	Turn turn
	Blast blast
	Screech screech
	Howl howl
Laugh laugh	Blast blast
Heal heal	Howl howl
Blow blow	
Stand stand	Turn turn
Beg beg	
Flesh flesh	Screech screech
Night	
Might	
Laughs	
Barfs	
Turbine machine iron cement	Thirst lament
Turbine machine iron cement	Aim bear
Aeroplanes cranes electricity	
Revolution lightening flash torch war	Hesitate hesitate
	Hesitate hesitate
Dare dare	
Dare dare	
Turbine machine iron cement	Revolution turn turn
Discourage encourage shard the thirst	Light the shining turn turn
Fümms bö wö tää Uu	
	Pögiff quii Ee.
Dedes nn nnrrrrrr	Iiiiiiii Eeeeeeee
M-pifffff tilfffff tooooooooooo	Tlllllllllll

Jüü-Kaa. *The Jüü is sung nearly an octave lower than the Kaa.*

Rinnzekete bee bee nnz krr müüü

Rackete bee bee.
Rumpftillfftoo?

Ziiuu ennze ziiuu rinnzkrrmüü!
Rackete bee bee,
Fümms bö wö tää zää Uu?

Revolution Lightning Torch War
War Torch Lightning and fire

Chase them away!

GROUP 1, 2   Turbine machine iron cement
Turbine machine iron concrete
War torch thunder lightning and fire
Justice Justice Justice!!!!!!!!!!!!

PJ

Ziiuu ennze ziiuu
   rinnzkrrmüü

Ziiuu ennze ziiuu
   nnz krr müü,

Rackete bee zee!!!
Uu zee tee wee bee
   FÜMMS!!!!!!

For Human Rights
& justice.
We're coming along!

1946   **The Family Plot**

          CHARACTERS
NORA	recently †
EMIL, her husband	†
HANS, her oldest son	†
FRITZ, her 2nd son	†
HEINRICH, her 3rd son	†
WILHELMA, her daughter	living
AIDA, her mother	†
WILHELM, her father	†
KARL, her stepfather	†
EILARDINE, Emil's mother	†
THE WELCOMING ANGEL	between life and death
BUNNY, Nora's friend	living
BUCKY, Nora's friend	living

I.
In the Family Crypt

It is dusk and a few candles are still burning from Nora's funeral, which has just taken place. Roundabout, sometimes atop each other, are the coffins of the buried dead. Today's funeral has brought a large number of wreaths and ribbons. The new coffin with Nora inside stands in the middle. In a corner are Bunny and Bucky, observing, talking together. The last of the funeral crowd are going up the steps. Wilhelma remains behind.

WILHELMA	*to Bunny* My poor dead mother, how miserable she must be feeling now.
BUNNY	She made everyone else feel miserable.
BUCKY	That was her nature, being miserable. She only felt good when someone else would suffer.
WILHELMA	But didn't it make you just cry, how the preacher praised her good nature, all the good things she did in her life.
BUNNY	I always did say Nora had two natures.
BUCKY	Two natures for sure. With the one she would giveth, with the other she would taketh away.

WILHELMA   But she didn't drive everyone off as ill-mannered as she was. You two for example have remained her truest friends.
BUNNY   So we did and we will always be her friends.
BUCKY   One can still be a friend to someone for all their wicked ways. Maybe one loves them just because they're wicked. We were always her good friends.
WILHELMA   Poor mother, how miserable she must be feeling. Now there's no one for her to be pestering. How sad and lonely she must be.
BUCKY   Well, one never knows, does one. Do you know what it's like beyond this life? Well, do you?
WILHELMA   Maybe there are other things they want then, maybe mother's feeling good now, maybe she wants to make the angels feel good too.
BUNNY   It doesn't happen all that quickly. A person cannot simply change her lifestyle when she dies. She will look for every chance to go on being as she was. Someone who lives to scheme and badger others while alive, surely will do that to the dead after she dies.
WILHELMA   But that can surely only be a passing phase. Surely she must be readied for eternity, even if she wasn't when she was alive.
BUCKY   I have always imagined the grave as that kind of preparation. The grave is a transition phase. An angel receives the dead and tests if they are ready for eternity. And if she isn't worthy to be saved, she has to wait. We hope your mother finds the circumstances in her favor.
BUNNY   And yet it's pretty sure she won't. It's pretty sure she'll have to wait.
WILHELMA   Mother was both good and bad. Maybe her bad side still can be forgiven.
BUCKY   Let's leave the dead alone for now, they want to be alone.
WILHELMA   Let me still look at all these wreaths and ribbons. How wonderful they are. Who has so many pretty wreaths after she dies?
BUCKY   Money can buy you anything.
WILHELMA   And so many mourners?
BUCKY   She had them all completely cowed.
WILHELMA   Whether she did or not, they came. But now we have to tear ourselves away. The dead have only this brief time for rest, in this their transitory life.

Wilhelma, Bunny, and Bucky go slowly off, and there are no longer any living beings in the crypt. Slowly, one after another, the dead climb from their coffins and form into groups. As starters

WILHELM   That's a real strain, to be locked in there for so long.

AIDA   *climbing out.* Yes, it *was* too long. The funerals in my time were considerably shorter. But I'm most anxious now to see what Nora looks like.

WILHELM   And what she'll sound like now. It's been a long time now since we last saw her.

KARL   That was at Franz's funeral, Wilhelm, wasn't that it?

WILHELM   I'm not talking to you. You disgust me.

AIDA   Oh, Wilhelm, why won't you finally give up this endless quarreling? Karl spoke to you in the most friendly way. Why was your answer to him so *un*friendly?

WILHELM   Me *un*friendly? I was hardly what you would call *un*friendly. What he did to me was clearly more *un*friendly.

KARL   What did I do to you?

WILHELM   You married my wife!

KARL   In legal terms that's absolutely true. She was a widow.

WILHELM   And so you went ahead and married her. So much for your squeaky clean morality. . . . And what becomes of me out in Eternity? In Eternity I have the right to be her lawful husband, without which legal right I lie here in this coffin underneath the two of you and have the damndest job to climb out for a breath of air.

AIDA   Get off it, you old goat. You know that we all like you and that I married Karl with you still in my mind. For me the two of you are equal. You know I love you and I always have.

WILHELM   You were unfaithful to me.

EMIL   I can't listen to this anymore. As long as I've been dead, the three of you go on and on about your marriages.

WILHELM   Well, thanks and no thanks. Or do you think it's so great to hear you keep on saying what a good wife Nora is?

EMIL   Yes, she was always good to me. She was my everything.

AIDA   Because you were a baby. You made her into what she was. A man who always says "yes" is a brown-nose.

EMIL   No, not a brown-nose, a man who feels safe in the love of his wife . . .

EILARDINE   A brown-nose! You're a weakling, son of mine. You always said "yes" to avoid a hell on earth. But you sacrificed us others.

EMIL   Mother, it was because I was so truly diplomatic that I made life easy for the lot of you.

EILARDINE   I wish that I had had a real son, not some gutless little pansy. Because however much I tried to make you strong, you always ran back to your wife.

EMIL   Mother, you should watch your tongue. You know all the harm you've caused me. Just think, when the Welcoming Angel comes, she'll be back with us and then she'll absolutely say what's on her mind.

EILARDINE   I'll spit in her face.

FRITZ   Now, Granny, that's a little much. Mother was always very good to you.

EILARDINE   Good to me? Good to me? When I was getting sicker and was needing medicine, she didn't give me not a single mark I needed. And my leg got swollen and more swollen till I died. I would like to spit just one more time on all your fancy company. She's got me on her conscience. It was she that did me in.

FRITZ   Granny, you have no idea of how frightened we children always were of getting punished. When you played the lion, you were good what with your single tooth and all, a lion with a single tooth, but when you talked to us, you were just awful.

EILARDINE   That's it, you always took your mother's side.

FRITZ   Because our mother was a better one than you.

EILARDINE   Better for you, you mean; she was just horrible for Hans and Heinrich.

FRITZ   Granny, play the lion just this once. This once.

EILARDINE   Me play the lion?

HANS   Oh, Granny, yes. We want to learn the true meaning of fear.

WILHELM   Don't you children ever intend to grow up? You aggravating bunch of whippersnappers! Day after day I have to hear about this cockamamie game. That this frail old woman, this hag, should play a lion!

EILARDINE   Stop it or else I'll play the lion now. I know how much you squeal with terror when I do it.

FRITZ   Play the lion, oh yes that's really great! Oh, Granny, do please play the lion.

THE WELCOMING ANGEL	Dear people, dear children, good evening. I am the Welcoming Angel. Has a new dead person arrived? A person named "Nora"?
WILHELM	Yes indeed. For there in her coffin she lies, neath a sprig of acacia, my dear daughter Nora. She is still in her death sleep.
ANGEL	And all of you, surely you all must be happy to have her among you again.
HANS and FRIEDRICH	Our mother, our wonderful mother.
FRITZ	Though with somewhat mixed feelings.
EMIL	How terrific, soon she'll be back with us.
WILHELM	I am her father, of course. She inherited my qualities.
AIDA	Just don't kid yourself about the weak points, you old drunk.
ANGEL	*steps up to new coffin* Nora, arise. *Beneath the flowers and wreaths there is a stirring, and Nora wriggles her way out.*
NORA	*assumes a stiff posture and thrusts out her right arm* Heil Hitler!
ANGEL	Nora, I am the Welcoming Angel. This is my processing station. And here we don't greet one another by saying "Heil Hitler."
NORA	Are you an S.A. Angel or an S.S. Angel? You should feel quite at ease about saying "Heil Hitler." This is my family grave and here we only allow the true German greeting "Heil Hitler."
ANGEL	Up in Heaven we still haven't gotten around to "Heil Hitler."
NORA	That will come to pass too if our Führer wills it.
ANGEL	Nora, here is where you must prepare to meet your savior.
NORA	I'm doing that too. I'm signed up in the women's frauenschaft.
ANGEL	In heaven we don't have a women's frauenschaft.
NORA	Then I'll start one for you. While we wait here, the Women's-Frauenschaft-Family-Grave-Detachment will do us just fine.
ANGEL	Then I think I'll start going.
NORA	Yes, go. We can set up our women's frauenschaft without you.
ANGEL	But there's the matter of your two little children. We let them spend the extra time here at the checkpoint so they could be here to greet you. Otherwise I'll have to take them with me.
NORA	Oh, little Hans and little Heinrich. Come over to your dearest mother. How I did sorrow for you when you first passed away. I let no day go by that I didn't bring flowers to your grave. You were the first ones in our family to lie there. That was a grave worth

	seeing. People drove for miles to see your darling grave, so pretty had I made it. Back then there wasn't all my Party work to do. Now will you take my children from me?
ANGEL	I hate to say it but your time with them is up. And I'll also have to take your husband with me.
NORA	Take him and good riddance. What a bore. Even before he died he used to sleep all day. And always had soup dribbling down his beard.
EMIL	Nora, I waited for you all this time. My heart is longing for you.
NORA	Sure you waited but would you sign up in the Party? No. Quibbling all the time and no constructive labor. Now you can wait a few more years in heaven. In the meantime I'll organize the women's frauenschaft down here. So go off with the Angel now and keep your napkin tucked in when you're eating. But tell me, S.S. Angel, why don't you also take my first son, Fritz?
ANGEL	Because he isn't on the list.
NORA	Then put him on it. He was a competent, excellent person. I always said it: if he had lived a little longer, he would have been another Goebbels. Then I could have given him a few good lines to say.
ANGEL	No, definitely not on it. But your mother-in-law is there.
NORA	Eilardine? That's clearly a mistake. She's got a spunky side to her and all, but she's a totally asocial creature. No schooling, no sense of the greater whole. Only would think about her belly. Not the sort you'd call on to make sacrifices. Her one thing was that she could play the lion, but a lion with no teeth, or just a single tooth, what was the point of it? A cat ought to show a whole mouthful of teeth.
ANGEL	Sorry if she's still got a lot in her character to work on, but she's coming with me.
HANS and HEINRICH	Then can she play the lion in heaven, every day, can she, Angel?
EILARDINE	I was actually looking forward to seeing Nora. We used to quarrel with each other in the past. I would have liked to keep it going here. But later, if Nora should come up to heaven, we can keep it going there.
ANGEL	You have to put an end to that once and for all. No quarreling in heaven.

EILARDINE	Good, then I'll stay here in the family crypt.
WILHELM	When are we getting out of here? No one can take this endless squawking any longer.
ANGEL	From what she says herself I'll have to let this lady stay behind, and you can't leave here either, no you're stuck here in your bodies until we set you free. But maybe on the basis of your marriage we can free you later on.
NORA	Mister Angel, you are really taking too much of my time. I have constructive labor still to do here, I have to organize our little Nazi chapter. Do please take your souls away. Hans, Heinrich, who else was there? Emil doesn't want to go with you and you don't want Fritz to go and Eilardine won't stay here. Everything is hunky-dory. So for now "Heil Hitler"!

Angel exits with Hans and Heinrich.

NORA	So let me welcome you now as the local group commander of the Women's-Frauenschaft-Family-Grave-Detachment. But first of all, the women! My dear mother, dear Aida.
AIDA	First time I ever heard you call me that. My dear mother?! And I don't have a clue as to what a women's frauenschaft is.
NORA	Deutschland, thou wast dead, e'er Hitler Deutschland led. And which of you did ever hear of Hitler?—None of you? Oh yes, my darling consort, Emil. And why are you not in the Hitler Youth, why, why?
EMIL	I was too old.
NORA	I can't accept that. No, you could have been some kind of office manager—in fact you should have been.
EMIL	I was too old to learn all that. In the Germany I lived in, there was still no Hitler, and then he came all of a sudden and he wanted to put everything in order, and I said, "Excuse me but I can't unlearn it all."
NORA	My darling Emil, you would have lived a much different life if I hadn't been there. The Nazis accepted that, your being old, because I fought for Hitler. And I will introduce the spirit of the nation here and now—whether you want me to or not! This will now become the official cell of the Emseder-Family-Grave-Cemetery Detachment of the German-National-Socialist-Party-Women's-Frauenschaft.

AIDA	What's the point of it?
NORA	The point, dear mother, is that we are here and now amalgamating.
FRITZ	We're *what*?
NORA	Not you, dear child, dear son. For you there must be another situation. We cannot have you in the women's frauenschaft. But maybe you can be the propaganda führer for the frauenschaft. I myself will give you lessons.
KARL	Could be interesting for once, hearing something different than Aida's getting married.
NORA	We two, she mother and I daughter, form the kernel, loosely speaking, of our women's frauenschaft.
WILHELM	Around which the fathers and the sons then cluster?
NORA	No. For you we'll work out something else. The newer members of our family will cluster around us, when they die.
FRITZ	That's just Wilhelma. She is the only one still living.
NORA	Then she will do. We have no need for any more than her.
FRITZ	Could you provide a few more details?
NORA	We will offer up our lives and deaths in service to our leader.
WILHELM	Who is our leader?
NORA	Adolf Hitler.
KARL	Where does he lead us?
NORA	Unto Greatness.
FRITZ	What can we do there?
NORA	Help him.
AIDA	How can we help him? We no longer have connections with the living.
WILHELM	She's right, you know. How can we help him?
FRITZ	I'd be glad to help, but how?
NORA	It's very simple. We here are a small but tight-knit unit, who from this family grave shall raise our banner high. But we will someday come into our own. What can a single person do? Nothing. What did the others do, there in their lives on earth? As little as it was, they bore the burden of the spirit and stomped morality into the ground. We are the 5th Column of the Emseder-Family-Grave-Detachment.
FRITZ	And for what are we the 5th Column?

NORA	For Heaven. We will take the morality of the angels and will trample it until it falls to pieces. In place of God we'll worship Hitler in our Heaven, and God will end up in a concentration camp. Heil Hitler.

II.

The same family crypt. Wilhelma has just been buried. Bunny and Bucky remain behind and talk together.

BUNNY	Poor Wilhelma, what she had to put up with from those Nazis. Any freedom-loving, tyrant-hating person would surely have died from it, especially to see her Fatherland oppressed by Nazis.
BUCKY	Scarcely anyone as eager for their downfall.
BUNNY	And she had to stand by and watch how just because of them her dear old Germany was totally demolished.
BUCKY	Hannover a pile of ruins. Berlin near wiped out. And they wouldn't let her say what she was feeling.
BUNNY	And when the liberation came, when she was free to speak at last, Death came and took away her life.
BUCKY	May she find peace out in that other world. At least she had the happy news that National Socialism was totally demolished.
BUNNY	Dear Wilhelma: we pray you have a well-earned rest, a well-earned happiness with your own kind in Heaven.

Bucky and Bunny go up the steps. One by one the dead come out of their coffins.

NORA	What a sloppy bunch! Emseder women, let's snap to it. Get a move on, Eilardine.
EILARDINE	Well, pardon me! I have to pull my bones together first.
NORA	You haven't changed one bit, in all the time I've known you, you go on sassing me and sassing the new order Hitler gave us. Now pay attention to my message of the day. We are here paying homage to our great and brilliant leader, he who has led us Germans out of wretchedness to freedom. Before him all our enemies do sink into the dust, such glory and such greatness does he bring to Deutschland. Let us support him now with all our powers. Yea, let us conquer Heaven for him through our works, and, if it must be, may we yet triumph in peace through force of arms. Heil Hitler!

ALL	Heil Hitler — — —
	Fritz, Emil, Karl, and Wilhelm come out slowly while she speaks.
NORA	You could have waited a little longer before coming out. We're having a little Hitler party here and you really mustn't bother us.
FRITZ	Day after day the same crappy slogans. Right now I'm waiting for my sister.
ANGEL	*flies in slowly from the side* Dear friends, once more we have a new arrival. Our own Wilhelma.
	He opens the coffin. Wilhelma steps out.
NORA	Achtung! *The women snap to attention and shout* Heil Hitler!
WILHELMA	What *is* that? I thought I was finally free of that old war cry.
NORA	My dear daughter, we don't have anything more wonderful to say to you than Heil Hitler! With those two words we lay our souls down at your feet.
EILARDINE	You had better believe it.
AIDA	I was so happy being with you.
WILHELMA	You were always my dearest grandmother.
EILARDINE	And I wasn't?
WILHELMA	You too, I would never say anything against you.
FRITZ	And wasn't I your loving brother? If I had lived I would have been an office manager.
WILHELMA	I would have loved you even if you had no title.
NORA	Helma, just control yourself, we all can hear you. What would Emil say?
WILHELMA	Well, I'll repeat it for him if he didn't hear the first time.
NORA	You were always willful. You saw all the good things Hitler had accomplished, but you wouldn't acknowledge them and only acted contrary.
WILHELMA	Mother, I told you again and again: Hitler was a disaster, but not just for Germany, for the entire world. Not for a minute did I believe in that gangster.
ANGEL	Just so, my child, no honest German could believe in Hitler.
EMIL	I didn't believe in him either.
WILHELM	The first we knew about Hitler was when your mother died. I can tell you we've had it up to here. This little creep who said he'd make things better. Got to listen to it day and night, and then she's got them marching through the crypt, when there's no room for it. I can't stand the words Heil Hitler any more.

WILHELMA	You're absolutely right.
NORA	My own daughter says that!
WILHELMA	Hitler is dead.
NORA	Dead? Can that be true? Why wasn't he brought here with us?
WILHELMA	He's buried underneath Berlin. Near burnt to ashes.
NORA	Oh what a tragedy. Or was it deliberate, a crime—?
WILHELMA	His crime against the German people came back to crush him. And it will also take revenge against his party. They're waiting for a verdict now in Nuremberg.
NORA	Why doesn't the German nation rise up like a single man?
WILHELMA	The nation is defeated, and it's lucky to have been defeated, because the victory of our enemies is good luck for the German nation. To get rid of this Nazi disaster . . .
NORA	You mean the Nazis are defeated?
WILHELMA	Defeated. Yes. And Germany is pretty much destroyed.
NORA	But that can't be. Germany is on the verge of Hitler's 1,000-year florescence.
WILHELMA	His thousand years are over.
NORA	Have I led the Emseder-Women's-Frauenschaft-Detachment for a thousand years then?
WILHELMA	No. The 1000 years was just a hoax. Hitler only muzzled Germany for 13 years. Now it's free.
NORA	But even if Hitler's Germany is gone, there's still a women's-frauenschaft-detachment. No one can kill it off, because it's made up of dead people.
FRITZ	I don't have no ties to any women's frauenschaft.
EILARDINE	I'm fed up not being allowed to speak the way I want, I'm pulling out.
EMIL	I was never a fan of Hitler's.
AIDA	I've done enough serving. Now I want to be free.
KARL	Thank God the oppression is over.
WILHELM	Keep your women's frauenschaft but leave me out.
NORA	All right. If there isn't any women's frauenschaft, there's still one loyal party member. I am that woman!
ANGEL	Heaven takes true joy in the courageous words you all have spoken. So all of you this day are coming with me into Heaven . . . all, I'm sad to say, except our Nora.

NORA	I don't want to go to your Heaven, not if I can't organize a party cell there. I couldn't stand the endless singing up in Heaven.
ANGEL	Better to sing and pray than to squawk a Heil Hitler.
WILHELMA	Mother, you'll be staying here alone. Do you see how long a stretch that means for you?
NORA	Better alone down here than astray with you in Heaven.
WILHELMA	If you really love me, come with us and give up what's been lost already.
NORA	A thing is only lost once you give it up.
WILHELMA	Hitler is dead.
NORA	And I am too.
ANGEL	What are you still waiting for?
NORA	I have time, I can wait a thousand years. 2000 maybe. And someday, when a Hitler comes again, I'll be the first to join the party. That's what I'm waiting for.

JR

1945–1947   **For Exhibition**

It is dripping down from the culture of an industrial city, and nothing is left but bones. White bones are right, left bones are red, and in the middle are beans and scones. There is no middle, there is a muddle. The wind rolls down the terrace under the street among the apples and prizes are grown up to nothing. There are terrifying flowers with poisoned lips crying for peace. But the war is over while the peace remains a futuristic leaf among the best pictures of Picasso. Picabia and his doctor greet the time abroad. They have time because they have got double British summertime.
   Aren't they lucky?
      ATOMBOMB

POETICS

1919

The Artists' Right to Self-Determination
Postface

Heavenworlds irontwirls, railroad station and Paul Steegemann. That is the reason why I decided to publish this collection of my poems, amen.

What does it mean to write poetry? $2 \times 2 = 4$ is not yet a poem. (The airline Syracuse, buttered bread, central heating.) It is very difficult to make poetic use of a statement. Stramm beat thousands, even millions. (Cleansing salts can be used for a wide variety of stomach complaints.) Stramm beat thousands, even millions. Stramm was the great poet. The importance of the Sturm in making Stramm known is very. The importance of Stramm for poetry is very.

Abstract poetry.

Abstract poetry plays off values against values. One can also say "words against words."

That doesn't create meaning but rather a worldfeeling, and that is what matters. (The rabble has to show respect and obedience to every officer.)

Translation of the artist's worldview. (Bunion treatments in a society at peace, war merchandise.) Total experience greens the brain, but what matters is the shaping.

Rhyme, rhythm, and ecstasy must never become mannered. (With the advent of darkness those same ones are completed at no extra cost, thus only a single edition.) That is abstract poetry.

Merz poetry is abstract. In analogy with Merz painting it uses as given parts complete sentences from newspapers, billboards, catalogues, conversations, etcetera, with or without changes. (That is terrible.) These parts do not have to fit in with the meaning, because there is no more meaning. (That is also terrible.) There are no more elephants either, there are only parts of the poem. (That is terrible.) And you? (Design war loans!) Determine for yourselves what is poem, what is frame.

I owe a lot to Anna Blossom. I owe even more to the Sturm.

The Sturm was the first to publish my best poems and to show a collection of my Merz paintings.
    Greetings to Herwarth Walden!

Kurt Schwitters

The change from the old heavy pince-nez to the new, elegant finger-lorgnette for everyone a facial decoration.

PJ

1920   **From *Merz***

Today even the striving for expression in a work of art seems to me deleterious to art. Art is a primordial concept, exalted as a godhead, inexplicable as life, indefinable and pointless. The work of art comes into being through the artistic evaluation of its elements. I know only how I do it, I know only my materials, from which I take, I know not to what end.

The material is as unessential as myself. The only essential thing is giving form. Because the material is unessential, I use any material the picture demands. By harmonizing different types of materials among themselves, I have an advantage over mere oil painting, for besides playing off color against color, I also play off line against line, form against form, etcetera, and even material against material, for example wood against burlap. I call the worldview from which this mode of artistic creation arose "Merz."

The word "Merz" had no meaning when I formed it. Now it has the meaning which I gave it. The meaning of the concept "Merz" changes as the insight of those who continue to work with it changes.

Merz wants freedom from all fetters for the sake of creating artistic form. Freedom is not dissoluteness, but the result of strict artistic discipline. Merz also means tolerance toward any limitations based on art. Every artist must be permitted to compose his picture from nothing but blotting paper, for example, provided he can give it form.

The reproduction of natural elements is not essential for the work of art. But inartistic representations of nature, as such, can form parts of a picture if they are played off against other elements of the picture.

To begin with I concerned myself with other genres, for example with the art of poetry. The elements of poetry are letters, syllables, words, sentences. Poetry arises from the playing off of these elements against each other. Meaning is only essential if it is to be used as one such factor. I play off sense against nonsense. I prefer nonsense, but that is a purely personal matter. I pity nonsense, because until now it has been so neglected in the making of art, and that's why I love it.

Here I must mention dadaism, which cultivates nonsense just as I do. There are two kinds of Dadaists, the kernel and the husk dadas, the latter living principally in Germany. Originally there existed only kernel Dadaists, the huskdadaists peeled off from this original kernel under the leadership of Huelsenbeck[1] and in the split took part of the kernel with them. The peeling off happened amid loud howls, singing of the "Marseillaise," and distribution of kicks with foot and elbow, a tactic which Huelsenbeck still uses today. Under Huelsenbeck dadaism became a political affair. The well-known manifesto of the German Central Committee of Revolutionary Dadaists demands the introduction of radical communism as a dadaistic dictate. Huelsenbeck writes in his history of dadaism, published in 1920 by Steegemann: "Dada is German bolshevism." The above mentioned Central Committee Manifesto further demands "the most brutal fight against Expressionism." In his *History of Dadaism* Huelsenbeck also writes: "Anyway, art should get a sound beating." In the introduction of the recently published Dada Almanach Huelsenbeck states: "Dada carries on a kind of anti-culture propaganda." Huelsendada is clearly politically motivated and is directed against art and culture. I am tolerant and let everybody have his own view of the world, but I have to mention that such views are alien to Merz. As a matter of principle Merz strives only to create art, because no man can serve two masters.

But "the Dadaists' conception of dadaism varies greatly," as Huelsenbeck himself has to admit. And thus Tristan Tzara, the leader of the kernel Dadaists, writes in his 1918 Dada manifesto: "Everyone makes his own kind of art," and further on: "Dada is the billboard of abstraction." I have to mention that Merz entertains a close artistic friendship with this version of kernel dadaism and with the art of kernel dadaists like Hans Arp, of whom I am particularly fond, Picabia, Ribémont-Dessaignes, and Archipenko. In Huelsenbeck's own words, husk dadaism "has made itself into God's clown," while kernel dadaism holds fast to the good old tradition of abstract art. Husk Dada "foresees its own demise and laughs about it," while kernel dadaism will live as long as art itself. Merz too strives after art and is the enemy of

1 [Translator's note: Hülse (Huelse) means husk in German.]

kitsch, even of kitsch-as-principle, though the latter may call itself dadaism under Huelsenbeck's leadership. Not everyone who lacks the ability to judge art should be entitled to write about art: "quod licet jovi non licet bovi." Merz energetically and as a matter of principle repudiates Mister Richard Huelsenbeck's inconsequential and dilettantish views on art, while it officially recognizes the above-stated views of Tristan Tzara.

I should clear up another misunderstanding that could arise through my friendship with certain kernel Dadaists. It might be thought that I consider myself a Dadaist, especially as the word "Dada" appears on the cover of my collection of poems entitled *Anna Blume*, as published by Verlag Paul Steegemann.

The same cover has drawings of a windmill, a head, a locomotive running backward, and a man hanging in the air. This only means that in the world in which Anna Blossom lives, in which men walk on their heads, windmills turn, and locomotives run backward, Dada also exists. So as not to be misunderstood I have written "antidada" on the outside of my Cathedral. That doesn't mean that I am against dadaism but that in this world there also exists a movement directed against dadaism. Locomotives can run in both directions. Why shouldn't a locomotive run backward for a change?

As long as I paint, I also model. At present I am making Merz sculptures: Lustgallows and Cultpump. Like the Merz paintings, the Merz sculptures are made from various materials. They are conceived as round sculptures and can be looked at from all sides.

Merz House was my first architectural Merz work. Spengemann comments on it in issue 8–10 of *Zweemann*: "In Merz House I see a cathedral: *the* cathedral. Not a church building, no, but the building as truly spiritual conception of that which raises us into the infinite: absolute art. This cathedral cannot be used. Its inner space is so filled up with wheels that people cannot find room in it . . . this is absolute architecture with an exclusively artistic meaning."

To busy myself with various genres was for me an artistic need. The reason for it was not so much a desire for a widening of the scope of my work, but rather the endeavor to be an artist and not a specialist in one genre. My aim is the total Merz art work, which combines all genres into an artistic unity. First I married off single genres. I pasted words and sentences together into poems in such a way that their rhythmic composition created a kind of drawing. The other way around, I pasted together pictures and drawings containing sentences that demand to be read. I drove nails into pictures in such a way that besides the pictorial effect a plastic relief effect arose. I did this in order to erase the boundaries between genres. The total Merz art work is, however, the Merz stage, which so far I have been able to work out only theoretically. The first public statement about it appeared in the eighth issue of the *Sturmbühne*: "The Merz stage serves for the performance of the Merz stage work. The Merz stage work is an abstract work of art. As a rule, drama and opera arise from a written work, which in itself is already a complete work even without a stage. Stage set, music, and performance serve only as illustrations of this text, which is itself the illustration of an action. In contrast to drama or opera, all parts of the Merz stage work are inseparably linked; it cannot be written, read, or heard, it can only be experienced in the theater. Up until now one has differentiated between stage set, text, and score in theater productions. Each part was elaborated separately and could thus also be enjoyed separately. The Merz stage knows only the fusion of all the parts into the total work. Materials for the stage set are all solid, liquid, and gaseous bodies such as white wall, man, barbed-wire fence, water stream, blue distance, light cone. Use surfaces that can become solid or dissolve into gossamer meshes, surfaces that can fold like curtains, shrink or expand. Let things turn on themselves and move; let lines broaden into surfaces. Parts will be inserted into the set while other parts will be removed. The materials for the score consist of all sounds and noises that can be created by violin, drum, trumpet, sewing machine, ticking clock, water stream, etcetera. The materials for the text are all experiences that excite the brain and the emotions. These materials are not to be used logically in their objective relationships, but only within the logic of the work of art. The more intensively the work of art destroys rational objective logic, the greater the possibilities of artistic form. Just as in poetry word is played off against word, so in this instance one will play off factor against factor, material against material. Imagine the stage set as a kind of Merz painting. The parts of the set move and transform themselves, and the set lives its own life. The movement of the set can be silent or accompanied by noise or music. I demand the Merz stage. Where is the experimental stage?

"Take giant surfaces, conceived as infinite, cloak them in color, twist and push them around menacingly, disfigure their smooth shamefulness. Bend and turbulate finite parts, shatter drilling parts of nothingness infinitely together. Glue over smoothing surfaces. Wire up lines, movements, true movement climbs actual rope of wire mesh. Flaming lines, crawling lines, surfacing lines crossed. Let lines fight among themselves and caress themselves in giving tenderness. Let points burst like stars in between, dance in circles, and realize themselves into lines. Bend the lines, crank and crook angles strangling whirls around a point. In waves of whirling storm a line roars past, prehensile as wire. Sphere the spheres whirling air touch themselves. Penetrating each other disunite surfaces. Boxes edged up, straight and crooked and painted. Collapsible top hats disappear into themselves strangle boxes, crates. Posit lines pulling drawing a net ultramarining. Nets contain narrow the pain of Antonius. Let nets billow and swell, run out into lines, thicken into surfaces. Net the nets. Let veils flutter, soft folds fall, make cotton drip and water spray. Hurl air softly and white through thousand-candled arc lights. Then take wheels and axles, hurl them up and let them sing (Watergiant holdover). Axles dance mid-wheel roll spheres barrel. Ratchet wheels sense ratchets, find a sewing machine that yawns. Screwing upward or hunkered down, the sewing machine beheads itself, feet up. Take a dentist's drill, a meat grinder, a trolley scraper, buses and automobiles, bicycles, tandems and their tires, even wartime ersatz tires, and deform them. Take lights and deform them in the most brutal manner. Let locomotives crash into each other, let curtains and portières, spidernet threads and window frames dance and break groveling glass. Explode steam boilers to make railroad smog. Take petticoats and the like, shoes and wigs and ice skates, and throw them in the right place, where they belong, and do it always at the right time. Also take, and why not, man-traps, automatic pistols, infernal machines, the tin fish, and the funnel, everything of course in an artistically deformed state. Rubber hose is highly recommended. In short, take eveything from the elegant lady's hairnet to the emperor's screw, always according to the dimensions required by the work.

"Even people can be used.

"People can be tied to backdrops.

"People can also appear actively, even in their daily situations, can talk on two legs, even in coherent sentences.

"Now begin to wed these various materials to one another. Marry for example the waxed tablecloth to the home owners' stock company; bring the lamp cleaner into a relationship with the marriage between Anna Blossom and A-natural, concert pitch. Feed the sphere to the surface and let a cracked corner be utterly destroyed by 22-thousand candle power arc light. Let people walk on their hands and carry hats on their feet, like Anna Blossom. (Cataracts.) Foam is sprayed.

"And now comes the lava of musical saturation. Behind the stage set organs sing and say: "Fütt, fütt." The sewing machine screeches ahead. From behind a backdrop a man yells: "Bah." Another one appears suddenly and states: "I'm stupid." (Reproduction by any means strictly prohibited.) A clergyman kneels upside down among them and loudly calls and prays: "O mercy swarms distounds hallelujah boy, boy espouses drop of water." A waterpipe drips unchallenged monotone. Eight.

"Drums and flutes flash death, and a trolley conductor's whistle shines brightly. A jet of ice cold water in a pot runs down over the back of the man perched on the backdrop. He sings C-sharp D, D-sharp E-flat, the whole of the workers' song. A gas flame has been lit under the pot to boil the water and a violin melody shimmers pure and tender as young girls. A veil overwidens widths. Deep darkred the middle boils embers. Something stirs gently. In waves arise long violin sighs and expire. Light darkens stage, even the sewing machine is dark."

Meanwhile this publication aroused the interest of the actor and theatrical director Franz Rolan who had kindred ideas, namely to make the theater independent of the playwright and to let the performances grow out of the available materials of the theater: stage, backdrops, color, light, actors, director, painter, and public. Together we have thoroughly worked through the idea of the Merz stage in relation to its practical application, theoretically for the present. This has turned into a voluminous manuscript that will soon be ready to go to print. Maybe later on we will also have the occasion to witness the total Merz work of art. Create it ourselves we cannot, because we too would only be parts of it, mere material.

PJ

1922

i
A Manifesto

Today every child knows what Merz is. But what is i? i is the middle vowel of the alphabet and the designation for the consequence of Merz in relation to an intensive apprehension of the art form. For the shaping of the work of art Merz uses large ready-made complexes that count as the material, to shorten as much as possible the path leading from the intuition to the actualization of the artistic idea, so as to avoid heat loss through friction. i defines this path as = 0. Idea, material, and work of art are the same. i apprehends the work of art in nature. Here the artistic shaping is the recognition of rhythm and expression in a part of nature. Thus no loss through friction, i.e., no disturbing distraction during creation occurs here.

I demand i, not as the only form of art but as a special form.

The first publicly available i-drawings can be seen in my May 22 exhibition in the Sturm Gallery. May I add, for the sake of the art critical gentlemen, that evidently a much greater ability is needed to cut out works of art from an artistically unformed nature, than to put together a work of art out of any kind of material based on one's own artistic law. Any material will do for art; it only has to be given form for there to be a work of art. But for i not all materials will do, as not every nature lets itself be cut out into an artwork. Therefore i is a special form. But it is necessary for once to be coherent. Can an art critic understand that?

PJ

1924   **Consistent Poetry**

Not the word but the letter is the original material of poetry: Word is:
1. Composition of letters.
2. Sound.
3. Denotation (Meaning).
4. Carrier of associations of ideas.

Art is inexplicable, infinite; for consistency of form its material has to be clear, unambiguous.

1. In a given word the sequence of letters is unambiguous, is the same for everyone. It is independent of the personal position of the observer.
2. The sound is unambiguous only for the spoken word. For the written word it is dependent on the observer's imaginative faculty. Therefore sound can only be material for the performance and not for the poetry.
3. Meaning is unambiguous only when the designated object is present. Otherwise it is dependent on the imaginative faculty of the observer.
4. The association of ideas cannot be unambiguous, as it is totally dependent on the combinatorial faculty of the observer. Everybody has different experiences and remembers and combines differently.

4. Classical poetry counted on the similarities between people. It considered the associations of ideas as unambiguous. It was mistaken. At any rate it built its foci on associations of ideas: "Über allen Gipfeln ist Ruh" ("O'er every mountain peace does reign"). Here Goethe does not only want to indicate that there is quiet on mountaintops; the reader is supposed to enjoy this peacefulness in the same way the poet, tired from his official duties and usually functioning in an urban environment, does himself. That such associations of ideas are not all that commonly shared can be shown if one were to read such a line to someone from Heidjer (a region of two inhabitants per square

kilometer). That person would certainly be much more impressed by a line like "lightning harry zigzags the subway crushes the skyscraper." At any rate, the realization that all is quiet does not bring forth poetic feelings in him because, for him, quietness is the normal state of affairs. The poet has to take poetic feelings into account. And what is a poetic feeling? The whole poetry of quietude rests and falls with the observer's ability to feel. Here words are not given their value.

Except for a very minor sound rhythm in the cadence, there is but one rhyme connection (between "Ruh" and "du") in the next verse. The only conforming relation between the parts in classical poetry is the one concerning the association of ideas, i.e., poetic feeling. The whole of classical poetry now appears to us as dadaistic philosophy, and its effects are all the crazier the less the intention to be dadaistic is present. Today only the couplet singers on Variety stages hark back to classical poetry.

3. Abstract poetry separated—and therein lies its great merit—the word from its associations, and played off word against word; more particularly concept against concept, while taking sound into account. That is more consistent than the evaluation of poetic feelings, but not yet consistent enough. What abstract poetry tried to achieve is achieved in a similar fashion, though more consistently, by dadaistic painters, who played off actual real objects by nailing or gluing them next to each other in a painting. Concepts can be played off against each other much more clearly this way than when their meanings have been translated into words.

2. Nor do I consider it to be very consistent to make the sound into the carrier of the poem, because sound is unambiguous only in relation to the spoken and not in relation to the written word. Sound poetry is consistent only in one case, namely when it is created in public performance and is not written down. One has to differentiate sharply between writing poetry and giving a poetry reading. For a reading, poetry is only material. The reading doesn't even care if its material is poetry or not. One can, for example, perform the alphabet, which was originally only a

utilitarian form, in such a way that it results in a work of art. Much could be said concerning artistic readings.

1. Consistent poetry is constructed from letters. Letters have no concepts. Letters in themselves have no sound, they only offer the possibility to be given sound values by the performer. The consistent poem plays off letters and groups of letters against each other.

PJ

1924–1925

What Is Madness?

Madness can be divided.
Madness can be divided and multiplied.
The best way to learn about madness is to distance oneself
   from it.
Madness is politics.
Dada is against politics because it is against madness.
Politics stand at the soft core of our time.
May that core soon soften further and may it leave our time
   free space for being free.

PJ/JR

1925   **Language**

The meaning and intentions of a new language are first realized when it is not only clear and understandable but cut down to the bone. What matters is the greatest possible simplification and compression.

We start out with some concepts

be (have)		*not be* (not have)
a		u

will (desire)	*fear*	*suspect*
o	i	e

The pronunciation of the vowels is long. When it's short, a *c* comes after the vowel.

In that case the verb is treated as an infinitive. Not all verbs begin with vowels.

Pronouns:

I	you	(he)	(she)	it	we	you (pl.)	they
b	d	m	n	g	p	t	k

The pronunciation of the consonants is flat, distinct, but minus vowels, the way that children learn in school.

The German alphabet is:

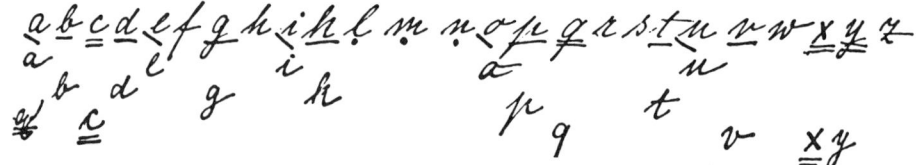

To start with, I only use a second letter as a kind of sign. A *c* after a vowel stands only for a shortening, a short sound, thus:

a e i o u (long)   ac ec ic oc uc (short)

The *c* thus turns into a glottal stop, a short occlusive sound, and so into a new sign: *c* by itself is spoken like the urge, the will to be a vowel.

The pronouns are placed before the verb

I am or I have	——————— ba
You (s.) are or you have	——————— da
He is or he has	——————— ma
She is or she has	——————— na
It is or it has	——————— ga
We are or we have	——————— pa
You (pl.) are or you have	——————— ta
They are or they have	——————— ka

I am not or I have not	——————— bu
You (s.) are not or you have not	——————— du
He is not or he has not	——————— mu
She is not or she has not	——————— nu
It is not or it has not	——————— gu
We are not or we have not	——————— pu
You (pl.) are not or you have not	——————— tu
They are not or they have not	——————— ku

I will	——————— bo
You (s.) will	——————— do
He will	——————— mo
She will	——————— no
It will	——————— go
We will	——————— po
You (pl.) will	——————— to
They will	——————— ko

The affirmative "yes" is expressed by	————————— ac = yes
and the negative "no" by	————————— uc = no or not
and the desiderative "will" by	————————— oc = desired, willed, wanted

With verbs the *not* is long, a *u* that gets tacked on

I will not [want not]	——————— bou
You (s.) will not [want not]	——————— dou
He will not [wants not]	——————— mou
She will not [wants not]	——————— nou

It will not [wants not] ——————— gou
We will not [want not] ——————— pou
You (pl.) will not [want not] ——————— tou
They will not [want not] ——————— kou

The pronunciation is like two sounds one right after the other. For emphasis you use a tacked-on *sh*-sound. I write it *x*, because *x* is a double stroke. And for deemphasis you use a tacked-on *l*. In this way many, very, much, good, and a lot are *sh*, while few or sort of is expressed by *l*.
Bash, for example, equals I am very much, i.e., I strongly feel myself existing. *Dush* expresses that you barely feel yourself existing. *Mosh* means: he wills or wants a lot.

JR

1926   **[What art is, you know . . .]**

What art is, you know as well as I do: it is nothing more than rhythm. And if that's true, I don't have to burden myself with imitation or with soul, but can modestly and simply give you rhythm, in any material whatsoever: bus tickets, oil paints, building blocks, that's right, you heard me, building blocks, or words in poetry, or sounds in music, or you just name it. That's why you mustn't look too hard at the material; because that isn't what it's all about. Don't look for some hidden imitation of nature, don't ask about expressions of the soul, but try, in spite of the unusual materials, to catch the rhythm of the forms and the colors. This has about as much to do with bolshevism as a flapper's hairdo. It is, however, the essence of all art, i.e., that every artwork throughout history has had to fulfill this primary requirement: to be rhythm, or else it isn't art.

PJ/JR

1926   **Grotesques and Satires**
for a gathering of my poems

Introduction:
This volume gathers grotesques and satires. In these compositions some kinds of relationships are naturally narrated with humor. Naturally only a reader who stands above such satirized relationships can understand the humor; conversely it may have been the reader himself who was being attacked. That's why there are always people in my audience who feel insulted, because no one likes to hear his own weaknesses exposed.
[fragment]

PJ/JR

1927   **Numbers**

zero	one	deuce	three	four	five	sex	seven	eight	nine	ten	eleven	onezero
+	I	L	⊦	⊥	)	⊢	C	T	X	Γ	?	I+

All numbers divisible by 2 have their last digit pointing to the right, none of the others do

             L   ⊥   ⊢   T   Γ   I+

All numbers divisible by 3 have a stroke in the middle of their last digit, none of the others do (only they are angled)

             ⊦   ⊢   X   I+

All numbers divisible by 4 have horizontal strokes in their last digit, none of the others do

                    ⊥   T   I+

All numbers divisible by 6 have horizontal strokes in the middle of their last digit, none of the others do

                                  ⊢   I+

All numbers divisible by 12 end with   +
                (0 = +)

oneone	onedeuce	onethree	onefour	onefive	onesix	oneseven	oneeight	onenine	oneten	oneeleven	twozero
II	IL	I⊦	I⊥	I)	I⊢	IC	IT	IX	IΓ	I?	L+

PJ

1927   **typography and orthography: small letters**

in the development of our time many things run parallel: the demands of the new age express themselves the same way in different fields. simple objectivity, clear quietness, breadth of perspective, therefore the summing up of parts into a whole, therefore utilitarian materials, therefore system in all things, these are the goals of our age, sprung from the new feeling for life which has been given us on the one hand by technology and on the other by the desire for a new style, for the style of this age.

arbitrariness does not reign here, rather strictest law and logical reasoning. it is not by chance that clothing has become simple and casual, that women have bob-cuts rather than long plaited tresses, that architects design their buildings functionally, without ornaments, but in beautiful proportions. our age is not far from perceiving the beauty of systems.

as part of this general trend, printing also needed to be reshaped. only those who hold on to the old at any cost, who deny any kind of development, who are incapable of seeing the larger patterns and connections, can perceive the new typography as the expression of a temporary mood or of a fashion, and do not feel the need of well-being that a systematic order brings.

the decision to use only small letters has 2 important reasons:

1) because it is more accurate than the usual way of linking small and capital letters, and

2) because it is more economical.

1) considered historically, the use of small and capital letters is a willful mix of two alphabets, and using only small letters corrects this mistake. until today no one has succeeded, in whatever type of writing, to equalize the differences between small and capital letters sufficiently to avoid the feeling of disproportion.

2) if one were to introduce small letter alphabets commonly, a child would need to learn only half the number of letters, the typesetter would be able to work much faster, the printer would

need to buy only half as many fonts, one would type that must faster, typewriters would be that much easier to build, etcetera.

why do we still hang on to the old plaited tresses of small and capital letters?

PJ

1927   **My Sonata in Primal Sounds**
Explanation of the Symbols

The letters used are to be pronounced as in German. A single vowel is short, two do not double the sound but make it long when it is the same vowel. If 2 identical vowels are to be spoken as two, then the word is separated at that place. Thus "a" as in "Schnaps," "aa" as in "Schlaf," "a a" is a double short a, etcetera; "au" is pronounced as in "Haus." Consonants are soundless. If they are meant to be sounded, the vowel that sounds them has to be added. Examples: "b, be, bö, bee." When repeated, the consonants b p d t g k z are spoken separately, thus: "bbb" is pronounced like three single "b's." When repeated the consonants f h l j m n r s w sch are not pronounced separately but are elongated, "rrr" is a longer rolling sound than "r."

The letters c q v x y are omitted. The letter z is maintained for reasons of ease. Capitals are only used for separation, for grouping, and for the easier recognition of sections, as first letters of lines, etcetera. "A" is pronounced as "a." *One may* underline in red what is to be spoken loudly and in black what is to be spoken softly. Thus a thick red line means *ff* (fortissimo), a thin red line *f* (forte), a thin black line *p* (piano), a thick one *pp* (pianissimo). Everything not underlined is *mf* (mezzo forte). Using letters and syllables as notes is also possible, when the tempo is steady, for example:

$$\frac{4}{4}\left|\begin{array}{c}Oo\\1\end{array}\right|\begin{array}{cc}bee\ bee & bee\ bee\ bee\\ 4 & 4\end{array}\left|\begin{array}{c}bee\\8\ 8\end{array}\right|\frac{3}{1}\left|\begin{array}{c}Oo\\1\end{array}\right|\begin{array}{cc}zee\ zee & zee\ zee\ zee\\ 4 & 4\end{array}\left|\begin{array}{c}\\8\ 8\end{array}\right|\frac{3}{1}\left|\begin{array}{c}Oo\\1\end{array}\right|\begin{array}{cc}enn\ ze & 1\\8 & 8\ 4\end{array}\left|\begin{array}{c}enn\ ze\ 1\\8\ 8\ 4\end{array}\right|\left|\begin{array}{c}Oo\\1\end{array}\right|\ldots$$

(slowly, evenly)

This would be another, less obvious way of notating the second movement. When the beat is free one may also use bar lines to stimulate the imagination. Numbers are used exclusively to indicate rhythm. Numbers, bar lines, and everything in parentheses are not to be spoken. To sum up, the letters that are to be used are: a ä au e ei eu i o ö u ü b d f g h k l m n p r s sch ch w z.

The vowels are: a e i o u ei eu au ä ö ü.

When the r's are to be pronounced singly, the following orthography is suggested: RrRrRrRrRr. The same goes for Schsch-Schsch, or LlLlLl, etcetera.

When the rhythm is free, paragraphs and punctuation signs are used as in ordinary language; when the rhythm is strict, bar lines, or other rhythmic notational devices are used to divide the writing space into equal segments, but there is no use of punctuation signs. Thus , . ; ! ? : are to be read only as tone color.

Of course the use of ordinary script with the letters of the old roman alphabet can only give a very partial suggestion of the performed sonata. As is the case with any notation system, many interpretations are possible. As with any reading act, imagination is required to read correctly. The reader himself has to work seriously if he really wants to learn how to read. Work improves the reader's receptivity much more than questions or thoughtless criticism. Only he who has understood everything has the right to criticize. It is better to hear the sonata than to read it. That's why I myself like to and often do perform my sonata publicly and will accept all invitations to organize a sonata evening. As it is not possible, however, to organize such evenings everywhere, I have recorded certain characteristic parts of the work. This record was published as MERZ 12 and can be ordered from the Merz Verlag in Hannover, Waldhausenstrasse 5, for 20 marks. The whole sonata lasts about 35 minutes.

General Explanations:

The first movement of my Ur Sonata is built like a rondo with the main theme being: "Fümms . . ." This main theme is partially borrowed from a poem by Raoul Hausmann which was written down as follows:

F M S B W T C U
P G G F
M Ü

and, as far as I'm aware, was originally nothing more than a type sample for a selection of fonts. With great imagination Hausmann made it into a performance, and as he was originally from Bohemia, he sounded it somewhat like this:

fümms bö wö tää zää uu
pögiff
mü

The "Kwiiee" from the first theme of the first movement is also based on Hausmann's

Q I E

The "De des nn nn rrrr," which I first wrote "D D S S N N R" arose from the word D R E S D E N. Maybe it is of interest to the reader how this came about, though it is of no interest to the work of art. The "rakete" is of course nothing else but the word Rakete (Rocket). In the second part, "P R A" is a conscious spelling of the name "arp" in reverse. The reference is to Hans Arp, the French Dadaist from Paris, not to the "allgemeine Relativitäts-Prinzip," the general principle of relativity. Arp is the founder of the magazine *ARP*. The "zät üpsiilon iks wee fau uu . . ." comes from a backward reading of the alphabet. All other sound connections are freely invented, suggested in part subconsciously by shortened inscriptions on company plaques or on printed matter, but especially by the interesting inscriptions on railroad switch towers which always sound so interesting because one has no way of understanding them. Now, I know perfectly well that explanations do not bring one closer to a work of art and that they only have historical or dadaistic value. In the final analysis my explanations are a document concerning the inexplicability of a work of art, or, as Raoul Hausmann puts it: "First comes art, then piano playing."

Now something concerning the structure. Just as the gathering of the themes and inspirations was dadaistic and arbitrary, so the inner logic, rigorousness, and consistency with which they are worked through and organized were implacable. The sonata consists of 4 movements, an introduction, a finale, and (as its seventh part) a cadenza in the fourth movement. The first movement is a rondo with four major themes, which have specific markings in the text of the sonata. You should easily sense how the rhythm can be strong or weak, loud or soft, tight or loose, etcetera. Any attempt to explain the fine points in the variations and elaboration of the themes would eventually become boring and could impair the reader's and listener's pleasure. And, finally, I am no high school teacher. Still, let me draw attention to the word-by-word repetition of the themes before each new variation in the first movement, to the explosive beginning of the first theme, to the pure lyric of the sung "Jüü-Kaa," to the strict military rhythm of the third theme which sounds totally masculine compared to the trembling, sheepishly tender fourth theme, and finally to the accusatory end of the first movement in the questioning "tää?" The second part is composed from the middle out. That it is to be sung you can see from the notations in the text. The largo is metallic and incorruptible, it lacks sentiment and all appeal to the senses. Note how the "Rinn zekete bee bee" and "ennze" recall the first movement. Note also the long "Oo" in the introduction as a foreshadowing of the largo. The third movement is a true scherzo. Note the quick succession of the 4 short themes: "Lanke," "trr gll," "pe pe pe pe pe," and "Ooka," which are very different from each other, which is what creates the bizarre form so characteristic of a "scherzo." Themes 1 and 2 are unchangeable and return stubbornly with their rhythms. The "rrmmp" and "rrnnff" recall the "rrmmpff tillff too" of the first movement, though the sound now is no longer sheepishly tender, but short and commanding, very manly. Nor does "Rrumpfftillftoo" in the third movement sound as tender any longer. The sound of "ziiuu lenn trll" and "lümpff tümpff trill" derives from the main theme "lanke trr gll." The "ziiuu iiuu" in the trio strongly recalls "ziiuu ennze" from movement 1, except that here it is solemn and ceremonial. The scherzo is essentially different from the other three movements in which the long "bee" is extremely important. No "bee" occurs in the scherzo. The fourth movement is the most rigorous and structurally the richest. Again, the four themes are clearly indicated in the text.

Please pay attention to the block up to "Oo bee," which is repeated verbatim. There follows a long working through with many surprises, and finally the block reappears slightly transformed, only in that the order of the themes has changed. The transitional theme "Oo bee" distantly recalls the second movement. The long quick fourth movement is an excellent lung test for the performer, especially as the endless repetitions, so as not to sound too monotonous, often demand a major raising of the voice. In the finale I would like to draw attention to the intentionally inverse sounding of the alphabet from z back to a. One senses this and waits with much expectation for the a. But twice it ends painfully with b. In this arrangement the b sounds painful. In the third alphabet the calming resolution brings the a. But now a final and fourth repetition of the alphabet ends very painfully on "beeee?" This has permitted me to avoid the banality, which was close at hand, of putting the absolutely necessary resolution at the end. The cadenza is ad libitum, and every performer can put together his or her own cadenza, based on the themes of the sonata. I have limited myself to proposing *one* possible version for a performer lacking imagination. I myself perform a different version each time, which allows the cadenza—as the rest of the piece is performed word for word—to sound especially alive and to create a strong countermovement to the more rigid part of the sonata.

So there.

PJ

1929

About me by myself

Questions which are important to some people are absolutely unimportant to others. It is of no importance to me that I am a painter; it is, however, important that I have a profession, in which I can create and work. And I believe if I had become an engineer, I would have been quite satisfied with my calling, and if, for example, I had had to be a teacher I certainly believe that I would have worked for reforms in the schools, by which I would certainly have made myself as disliked as I am now for my painting and poetry. Therefore humanity should be happy that I became just an artist.

From the future I expect really nothing, for our earth has a thousand centuries of development behind it, and there is no reason to believe that out-and-out idiots have conducted the affairs of mankind. I am also quite inclined to say in this connection that mankind around me, as to normal gifts, is many times as gifted as I am. If however in spite of this it often seems that one were shut up in a mad-house . . . it is my opinion that many cooks spoil the broth and that they will always do so in the future. If humanity would, once and forever, decide to place its fate in my hands, I would guarantee it heaven on earth. But I fear that it will never do this, so alas, humanity, through no fault of mine, will, have to remain in the befogged state in which it now finds itself.

The happiest moment of my life was when I discovered that everything is really indifferent, for through that I won the freedom to work only as much as was necessary to satisfy my impulse to work. I remark at the same time, to my regret, that hunger is one of my impulses; and for this reason I often have to work more than my health can stand.

The unhappiest moments of my life for me, not for others, are those in which I have to do something that I have absolutely no desire to do, and I might say that for me, not for others, in such cases there is nothing in the work.

I consider it my greatest strength that I work in spite of the fact that many times I have no desire to work, and when it is very often useless, and I consider it useless because the future will treat it just as it treats old junk, as I treat the work of the past, unless it can put something better in the place of it. In every case and before all things I strive for results, for even if the striving is of no account, nevertheless the result is important, as the one way of knowing exactly what one has created.

I cannot say that I have ever liked one thing more than another, whether it be ideas or objects, for to me objects are only a means of expression and live for me in their form.

It would be quite banal to mention that obviously I should rather eat a ripe apple than a sour one. And it is quite a private matter, for instance, that I prefer guinea-pigs to white mice, because guinea-pigs are often quite droll to watch, while white mice are always stupidly turning in circles just like the whole of humanity, and the old mice are often bald just like men in the prime of life. Then I like salamanders very much, they have a noble repose, they do not spin about in circles, but lie in the damp, eat angleworms, above all things they shed their skins more often than men.

The art of today is a remarkable affair. In so far as it is art, it differs in nothing from the art of the past. In so far as it is not art, it differs just as little from the bunk of the past. Art is above all only formation, creation. Therefore it does differ from the growth of a plant or of a crystal, from the life of a star or the construction of a machine. Raoul Hausmann once very rightly said, "first art and then piano-playing." It is not to be inferred that all that is called piano-playing is art. And so we have, for example, in abstract painting today, in my opinion, the highest development that painting has had in the course of a thousand years, while the music of our day lags far behind that of Beethoven and Bach.

Of my world-view I have already spoken. I seem to myself to be a completely thinking man who, with other more or less thinking men, and a multitude of absolutely idiotic individuals, is shut up in a sort of insane asylum, in which one passes the time reading classic poetry. If any one asks me why I go on living in this madhouse, I can give him the same answer as to the question why I have visited that museum where "the lemon trees bloom": in order to observe and to register. Ecco.

I could here once more write ecco, but enough and why should one give oneself unnecessary labour.

1934 **Stone upon stone is a building**

Stone upon stone is a building.
But not as sum, building is form.
Building is form out of mass and space.
The hands create the form and give it color. Though they give more: Time.
Creating hands give to space everything the person who creates it, is: His world.
In the form, the play of forms, of colors, of images, of laws, yes, even of the things that are not named in the building, time lives in space for all times. Thus space becomes a parable for time and points toward eternal creation.

PJ

1946   **Present Inter Noumenal**

Poetry does not serve any more for needs
Since four thousand years it has served feudal archetypes
Since Homer, Aeschylos, Sophocles, Vergil, till Racine, Molière, Shakespeare, Goethe and Hugo, it has served to revive the great EMPTINESS by a heroic IMAGINARY, in a metaphoric language
Poetry of the PRESENT has given up the asiano-mediterranian archetypes
It has given up the HEROS
Poetry of the PRESENT has found the new objectivity of things in the living space
It does not seek any more to explicate phenomenals, be they social or false philosophical
Poetry of the PRESENT does not spring out of fear, it has liberated itself of the world = agony and the ridiculously tragic keeping up of the cunning of struggle for eating
Poetry of the PRESENT understands its objects, the words, as agents of our living space
It gives back to the words and by the words the correspondances of the things before and outside their social and eugenic needs
The poetical (non-musical) sound creates complex dimensions: functional, temporal and numerical, it shows by these inter-relations the "coincidentia oppositorum" of the things by their own value
These values are no ware of social classes, nor of historical aspect
Poetry of the PRESENT is outside the restrained history, outside the coward anthropophagous and anthropomorphous utilisations
PRESENT Poetry aims at the relative life of untamed and non-classified functions, avoiding the false semblances
PRESENT Poetry is neither FOR nor AGAINST, neither classic, nor romantic, nor surrealistic
It integrates BEING and it IS
                    Poetry Intervenes Now
                    Presence Is New
Raoul Hausmann   PIN
27.xii.1946   *Kurt Schwitters*

1946　　　　**PIN**

A fancy
A thing of fan
The right thing of phan
World needs new tendencies in poeting and paintry
Old stuff is not able to lead further on
Muses ought to be whisked, when mankind will survive
In the very war creative whisky is fallen very dry
We will develop whisky spirit, because we see it with our ears and hear with our eyes
Our phantic drsls and rlquars are full of whisked away formal life
They overwhelm "modern poetry" by their new taste
Their phantic contents are so direct, that they are placed above the meanings of language at all
Language is only a medium to understand and not to understand
You prefer the language, when you understand by it things, which everybody knows by heart already. We prefer the language, which provides you a new feeling for new whiskers to come
Give up your human feelings and please go through our fan pin and you will know, that it was worth while.
　　　　　　　　　PIN
　　　　　The thing of phan—fan

CHRONOLOGY

INDEX OF TITLES

ABOUT THE

TRANSLATORS

CHRONOLOGY

1887	Born June 20 in Hannover
1908	Abitur (A-level exams)
1908–1909	Arts and Crafts School, Hannover
1909–1914	College of Art, Dresden
1915	Marries Helma Fischer
1917	Army service as a clerk in Hannover (March–June)
1917–1918	Mechanical draftsman in Hannover (as emergency relief worker)
1918	First collages: the invention of MERZ Beginning of friendships with Hans Arp and Raoul Hausmann
1919	First Merz painting First exhibit at the Sturm Gallery, Berlin (with Klee and Molzahn) First publications in the magazine *Der Sturm* (poems, prose poems, articles, illustrations) "Anna Blume"
1920	"Die Kathedrale" "Sturm-Bilderbuch IV" First works exhibited in "Société Anonym," New York
1921	Performance/reading with Raoul Hausmann in Prague
1922	"Anna Blume," second, enlarged edition "Die Blume Anna" "Memoiren Anna Blumes in Bleie, eine leichtfassliche Methode des Wahnsinns für jedermann" (Memoirs of Anna Blume in Lead, an Easy-to-grasp Method of Madness for Everyman) Participates in Dada convention in Weimar
1922–1923	Dada-Tour with Theo and Petro (Nelly) van Doesburg through Holland First contributions to the Dutch magazine "*i 10*"

1923	Founds *Merz* magazine
From c. 1923	Merzbau (Merz Tower) in Hannover Freelance ad consultant and commercial artist
1927	Co-founder of the Modern Ad Design Group "Grosse Merzausstellung" (Merz Exhibit): German traveling exhibition
1929	Director of typography for Dammerstock Estates in Karlsruhe Participant in the exhibit "Abstract and Surrealist Painting and Sculpture," in the Kunsthaus, Zurich First trip to Norway
1930	Contribution to the magazine *cercle et carré* in Paris
From 1931	Annual summer vacations in Djupsvasshytta bei Seirvanger (West Norway, mountain country)
1932	Association with the group "abstraction création—art non figuratif" and contributor to the magazine of the same name Last issue (24) of *Merz*: "Ursonate"
From 1932	Annual vacations on Molde Island in the Moldefjord (West Norway)
1936	Participant in the exhibits "Cubism and Abstract Art" and "Fantastic Art—Dada—Surrealism" at the Museum of Modern Art, New York
1937	January 1, final emigration from Germany, settles in Lysaker near Oslo Nazi-sponsored Exhibit of Degenerate Art ("Entartete Kunst"): Schwitters' works removed from German museums Beginning of the 2nd Merzbau (destroyed by fire in 1951)
1940	April 9, escape from Oslo June 8, arrives in England
1940–1941	17 months in various British internment camps
1941	Settles in London

1943 Destruction of the Merzbau in Hannover

1944 Suffers a stroke

1945 Takes up residence in Little Langdale by Ambleside (Westmoreland, Lake District)
Grant from the Museum of Modern Art
Death of Helma Schwitters in Hannover

1947 Illness
Beginning of the 3rd Merzbau (Merz Barn) on Cylinders Farm, Little Langdale

1948 Dies January 8 in Kendal (near Ambleside)

INDEX OF TITLES

The numbers in parentheses following the entries in the index refer to the volume and page number where the original versions can be found in the Friedhelm Lach five-volume edition of Kurt Schwitters' work, *Das literarische Werk*, published by DuMont Verlag in Cologne between 1973 and 1981.

A-A Visual Poem (1, 201), 51
About me by myself (5, 321–323), 238
An Anna Blume (1, 58–59), 15
Analysis (1, 91), 46
And in the night (1, 157), 106
Anna Blossom Has Wheels (1, 150), 16
AO Visual Poem (1, 200), 50
Artists' Right to Self-Determination, The (5, 38–39), 213
At first men were limited (1, 163), 114
Augusta Bolte (2, 68–93), 137
Autumn (1, 92), 47
Autumn/The Last Fly (1, 102, 148), 88

Bahnhof, The (1, 65), 18
Banalities (1) and (2) (1, 172–174), 82
Buckets (2, 52), 136

Call It Killing You Off (1, 64), 17
Candle Fat (1, 87), 43
Chinese Banalities (1, 170), 32
Cigarren (1, 199), 40
Cnudgel (1, 49), 11
Consistent Poetry (5, 190–191), 223
Count Sardinowhocount (1, 160), 107
Critic, The, 37

Dadar (1, 161), 103
Decay's Way (1, 74), 26
Desire (1, 88), 42
Devil in Need (1, 116), 92
Die Gazelle zittert/The gazelle trembles (1, 177), 118
Difficult, 94–95
Dramatic Sketch (4, 23), 135
Dumb Poem (1, 89), 44

Esir, 94–95
Evening (1, 75), 27
Execution (1, 65), 18

Family Plot, The (4, 308–320), 197
Far away from (1, 162), 113
fishbone fish a fefishbone, A (1, 167), 115
Flight (1, 131–133), 96
Flower Like a Raven, A (1, 72), 25
For Anne: A Poem to Be Sung as a Round (1, 195), 93
For Exhibition (3, 301), 209
For Franz Marc (1, 84), 38
Four Bear Songs (1, 192–194), 89
[Frohe Tage] (1, 155–156), 104
From *Hannover Merzbau* (1, fig. 14), 85
From *Merz* (5, 76–82), 215
From the Back & from the Front to Start (1, 76), 28
Funeral Furnitures at your service (1, 52), 101

Great Ardor of Dada, The (1, 83), 38
Green Child (1, 45–47), 6
Grotesques and Satires (5, 250), 229

Hand, The (1, 91), 45
He She It (1, 56), 13
Herwarth Walden (1, 66), 20
High Fashion Furs (1, 81), 35

i (5, 120), 222
I and You (1, 154), 103
Ice Clocks (1, 89), 43
Ideas for Poems (5, 437), 87
If I Were, When I Was (1, 21), 94
Imagination (1, 152), 101
In the Middle of the World a House Stands (4, 85–87), 187
Indecent i-Poem (1, 94), 81

Königsberger Is Like That (1, 153), 102
Kurt Schwitters to the Swiss Dadaist Arp. Blackberries (2) (2, 47), 128

Language (5, 231–233), 226
Legborders (1, 44), 5
Light & Low (1, 50), 10
London Onion (1, 267–270), 108

Madd Madd World (1, 51), 12
Mai 191, 94–95
Mary the Red (1, 69), 23
Meadow, The (1, 82), 36
Murder Machine 43 (5, 288–292), 29
My Sonata in Primal Sounds (5, 288–292), 233

Nights (1, 40), 4
Numbers (5, 265), 230

On a Drawing by Marc Chagall (1, 70), 24
One day (1, 162), 112
[1 7 10] (1, 209), 86
Onion, The (2, 22–25), 121
Oon, 94–95
Opinion (1, 270), 111

p p p p p p p p p p (1, 95), 81
Perhaps Strange (1, 151), 99
Pin (1, 164–166), 116
PIN (5, 389), 242
Poem 25 (1, 204), 48
Portrait of Christof Spengemann (1, 68), 21
Portrait of Herwarth Walden (1, 67), 20
Portrait of Nell Walden (1, 67), 21
Portrait of Rudolf Bauer (1, 69), 22
Portrait of Rudolf Blümner (1, 68), 22
Premonitions (1, 68), 95
Present Inter Noumenal (5, 391), 241
Prisoner, The (1, 79), 33
Prisoner, The (1, 164), 114
Private Gentlemen, Attention Please! (1, 73), 25
Profane Words over the Eternal City (2, 345), 173

Quarter of the Feelings of Old Man Automato in His Ancestral Castle Atho, A (2, 58), 129

Raspberry Bonbons (1, 82), 36
Register (1, 208), 49
Repose (1, 57), 14

Roses abloom like daisy blossoms (1, 92), 46

Secret Drawer, The (2, 49–52), 130
Shadow Play (4, 26–31), 167
She Dolls with Dollies (1, 143), 102
She is my fairy queen (1, 159), 106
Shepherd's Play (4, 24–25), 165
Simile (1, 85), 41
Simultaneous Poem (1, 198), 14
Small Chinese Poem (1, 127), 96
S-S Visual Poem (1, 201), 51
Stone upon stone is a building (1, 120), 240
Subway Poem (1, 81), 35

There was a little Kew (1, 149), 100
"Thou" (1, 43), 5
[To avoid] (1, 160), 107
To Johannes Molzahn (1, 66), 19
To Maria (1, 69), 23
To the Berlin Proletariat! (1, 86), 42
Tortrtalt (1, fig. 10), 91
Twelve (1, 205), 47
Two Choruses from *Above and Below* (4, 89–91, 103–105), 191

Typographic Visual Poem (1, 200), 50
typography and orthography: small letters (5, 268–269), 231

Unstupid (1, 39), 3
Ur Sonata (1, 214–242), 52

Vexation Plays (4, 22–23), 134
Village Poem (1, 88), 44

Waggling (1, 75), 27
[What art is, you know . . .] (5, 244–245), 229
What Is Madness? (5, 200), 225
Wheelers Dealers (1, 74), 26
When someone once said (1, 125), 95
Wirecircus (1, 90), 45
Workers Song (1, 80), 34
World, The (1, 37), 3
Wound roses roses bleed (1, 48), 9

Your Most Humble (1, 64), 41

Z A (1, 205), 49

ABOUT THE TRANSLATORS

Jerome Rothenberg is the author of over fifty books of poetry, including *Poems for the Game of Silence*, *Poland/1931*, *New Selected Poems 1970–1985*, and *Khurbn & Other Poems* (all from New Directions). He has also edited six ground-breaking anthologies of experimental and traditional poetry (*Technicians of the Sacred*, *Shaking the Pumpkin*, *America a Prophecy*, *Revolution of the Word*, *Symposium of the Whole*, and *Exiled in the Word*) and has been actively engaged in poetry and performance since the late 1950s. Awarded the Before Columbus Foundation American Book Award in 1982, he is currently a professor of visual arts and literature at the University of California, San Diego.

Born in 1946, Pierre Joris left Luxembourg at eighteen and has since lived in the United States, Great Britain, North Africa, and France. He has published twenty books of poetry, including *Net/ Work* (Spanner Editions, London), *Breccia: Selected Poems 1972–1986* (Station Hill Press), and *Turbulence* (St. Lazaire Press), as well as several anthologies and many volumes of translations, into both English and French, the most recent being Maurice Blanchot's *The Unavowable Community* and *From the Desert to the Book* by Edmond Jabès (both from Station Hill Press). He currently teaches in the English department at the State University of New York, Albany.